My Writings: Personal Essays

Vol. 1

By
Colonel Ben L. Walton, US Army (Retired)
Foreword by Lawrence C. Coulehan, MD

Strategic Book Publishing and Rights Co.

Strategic Book Publishing and Rights Co., LLC
USA | Singapore
www.sbpra.com

For information about special discounts for bulk purchases please contact Strategic Book Publishing and Rights Co. Special Sales at bookorder@sbpra.net

ISBN: 978-1-946539-85-4

Table of Contents

Foreword

I am a board certified internist practicing in Denver, Colorado.

The first Walton I met was Ruth, Ben's wife. With her endorsement, Ben Walton became my patient and subsequently my friend.

In *Personal Essays*, Ben presents a series of themes meticulously researched and tempered by his eighty-six years of endurable experience. His wisdom, humor, and gentle sarcasm reminds me of Garrison Keillor's eclectic *Prairie Home Companion* radio program.

Included are personal topics such as his African American heritage, remarkable military career, aging, faith, and interpersonal relationships. He also touches on business practices, and even gives Albert Einstein some competition with his opinion about time.

After an easy two-hour read, I felt a bit better about myself, but knew I had a lot of homework to do. I'll listen a bit more to the music that comes from within and from the outside. I'll also have some quotes to share with my patients and friends.

Ben Walton is an outstanding writer. He would be equally effective on stage, in the pulpit, or on the air. He would be a perfect speaker to pep up a senior crowd.

Lawrence T. Coulehan, MD

Preface

*But I have yet to find a repository of general life advice and
observances which help people learn to navigate life in general. At
times, we all feel like life should come with an instruction manual,
but since it doesn't, I'm endeavoring to write one.*
—From http://mindwaste.com

Since retirement from the US Army in 1978, then completing over
twenty years in various day jobs during my second career as a civilian,
I've been a freelance writer. Make no mistake, I love to do two things
with equal order and precedence: read and write. The passion to do the
foregoing goes back to when I was ten years old and my teacher said,
"Benjamin," (later I shortened my name to Ben) "I admire how you
like to read and write. I'm going to help you." While I was in her class,
she often encouraged me to do both.

From 2000 to the present, I've penned hundreds of articles on a
multitude of different subjects. Many of them were printed in national
periodicals throughout the country. Additionally, I've written two
nonfiction books, *How to Be a Daily Winner and Feel Really Great!*
and *Great Black War Fighters: Profiles in Service*. The latter was
inspired by President John F. Kennedy's bestseller and 1957 Pulitzer
Prize-winning volume, *Profiles in Courage*.

Regarding motivation to create this volume, it came from three
sources: the Holy Bible; *Selected Essays, 1917 and 1932* by T. S.
Eliot; and *Things That Matter: Three Decades of Passions, Pastimes
and Politics* by Charles Krauthammer. Concerning God's word,
shortly after joining a Bible study group at a place where I worked in
the 1980s, I purchased *The Comparative Study Bible* (a parallel Bible
presenting the New International Version, the New American Standard
Bible, the Amplified Bible, and the King James Version). Since then,
I've had the habit of reading the word daily.

Concerning Eliot's work, a collection of prose and literary
compositions, his publication gave me ideas useful in the development
of *My Writings: Personal Essays*. Interestingly, one of the most ordered
books today on Amazon.com is Eliot's dated volume. With no intent to
take anything away from Eliot's work, the purpose of *My Writings* is
to provide information that resonates that readers can use effectively
in their daily lives.

About Krauthammer, a Pulitzer-Prize-winning syndicated columnist, political commentator, and physician, I was intrigued by his work because it was a collection of his columns, addressing varied topics, published in newspapers around the country over three decades. His work energized me to take on the daunting task.

To put this book in historical context, readers should know that for more than four hundred years, as documented in *The Art of the Personal Essays: Anthology from the Classical Era to the Present* by Phillip Lopate (author of three personal essay collections), this genre has been one of the richest and most vibrant of all literary forms in America for generations.

Also, based on history, *Essays by Michel de Montaigne,* the title of an assemblage of 107 essays written by him and published in 1580, astonishingly is rated by experts today as among the greatest nonfiction books of all time. Furthermore, Montaigne is credited with inventing the writing style of an essay, meaning a short subjective treatment of a given subject.

Lastly, this book aims to provide readers with a poignant and useful publication, worthy of their time, that is captivating, interesting, and stimulating, besides being a resource that will be treasured and passed on to later generations.

Ben L. Walton

Acknowledgments

This collection of essays are the best articles I've written from among hundreds of pieces that I've penned over twenty-five years as a freelance scribe. In developing the volume, I was motivated by three things, all related contextually. They are the Holy Bible, Abraham Lincoln, and Charles Dickens.

About God's word, it is mindboggling that the greatest book ever written was done reportedly by forty men who, by using the most primitive means, produced the Good Book. Thoughts about that awesome, monumental, and powerful accomplishment was really the catalyst for *My Writings: Personal Essays*.

Concerning Lincoln, it was this quotation that stood out was "I believe the Bible is the best gift God has ever given to man. All the good from the Savior of the world is communicated to us through this book."

Regarding Dickens, this comment, "The New Testament is the very best book that ever was or ever will be known in the world," was the internal impetus for the work.

Using divine influence, I assembled the most well-received essays, based on feedback from different sources, and took them to Lorel Westfall, a recommended word processor. Lorel took on the daunting task of typing and organizing the narratives, later producing the draft manuscript that was subsequently forwarded to the publisher. I'm deeply grateful to Lorel for her outstanding contribution to this project.

Finally, I would be remiss if I didn't dedicate this book to readers who have taken the time to pick it up and, hopefully, to read it. Make no mistake; at the eighty-seven-mile marker on life's highway, and to use a football metaphor, I'm at the two-yard line, with several minutes left on the clock before the game ends. This is the number one item on my bucket list.

Enjoy!

Introduction

To appreciate the contents of this book, it's worthwhile to know something about the author's early childhood and how the writer became a part of the clan.

In February 1930, the Walton family consisted of Grandpa Winger Vanhook, his daughter Florene Walton, who was married to Lem Walton, two boys, the oldest named Winger and the other Ira Lee. They were Lem's stepsons. In addition, there was Lemora, Lem's daughter from a previous marriage. All family members lived together in a house in Waco, Texas, except Lemora. Lemora was married to Jesse Taylor, a preacher who, with his wife, owned and managed the Waco Children's Home, a nearby orphanage.

Early one morning, a man and woman brought a baby boy to the orphan home. The child was no more than eight hours old, according to accounts. The family of the infant said they wanted to give up the boy for adoption.

Jesse and Lemora didn't have any children of their own. Moreover, Lemora didn't know anything about taking care of a baby, so she passed him to Lem and Florene, who immediately fell in love with the child. Shortly thereafter, they named the boy Benjamin Lee Walton.

Several years later, Lemora's husband died, and she moved to Dallas, Texas, to work, leaving Grandpa, Lem, and Florene to raised Benjamin. For a number of years, during summer months when school was out, Benjamin spent time with Lemora, returning later to his hometown. It was during one of those periods that he ran away for three months, returned to Waco, and weeks later enlisted in the Army at age seventeen. The rest is history.

LEMORA WALTON TAYLOR, CO-OWNER OF ORPHANAGE THAT RECEIVED
AUTHOR HOURS AFTER HIS BIOLOGICAL MOTHER GAVE BIRTH.

AUTHOR, AGE FIVE.

"Author with adopted family members: (standing on left) Florene, (seated, from left to right), Lem, Grandfather Winger Vanhook (Florene's dad), (on knees) author, (standing in second row) Lucele (wife of Winger), Winger, Ira Lee."

AUTHOR WITH WINGER WALTON.

AUTHOR WITH WINGER VANHOOK AND IRA LEE WALTON.

AUTHOR'S HOME IN WACO, TEXAS.

AUTHOR MEETS WITH IRA LEE WALTON
(BABENHAUSEN, GERMANY, 1965).

AUTHOR ENGAGED IN WRITING WORK (1976)

WRITING.

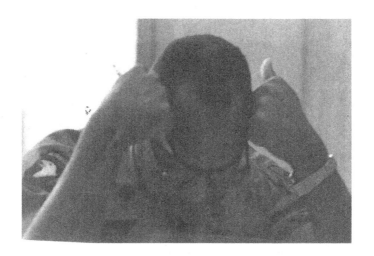

READING.

AUTHOR WALKING WITH NEWSPAPER.

PART ONE:
AGING

1

Aging Facts

Research reveals the following facts about people growing old:

1. Life expectancy is increasing at a faster rate. Between 1900 and 1960, life expectancy increased by 2.4 years, but since 1960, it has grown by 3.5 years.

2. In 2009, there were 39.6 million people aged 65 and older. Now there are over 40 million.

3. Minorities make up almost half of the older population. Forty-two percent of people 65 and older in the US are part of minority groups.

4. Many of the elderly are poor or close to it: 16.8 percent of the old folks in America are poor or destitute.

5. There are more people over age 60 than under 15.

6. About half of the employed elderly work full time. Of those who are working past 65, 55 percent work full time.

7. There are nine million elderly veterans over 65.

8. Fifteen million older people work as volunteers. Nearly half of all adults 65 or older work as volunteers in their communities.

9. Nursing home care costs average about $60,000 a year, depending on where the person lives in the US.

10. The elderly vote more than any other age group. Seventy percent of citizens 65 and older have voted in recent elections.

11. Twenty percent of seniors suffer from depression, twice the rate of younger adults.

12. Alzheimer's is spreading rapidly. Every minute and a half, a person in the US develops the disease, especially women.

13. Sixty-six percent of Americans 75 or older are in good health. The difference reportedly are in fair or poor health at the same age.

14. A bad childhood can shorten a senior's life. Those who face trauma as a child will typically age earlier than those who didn't.

15. Drivers over 65 have fewer accidents per person than those under the same age.

16. Elderly people who worry about falling over tend to fall over more often than those who don't.

17. Active older people live longer. Therefore, working past retirement can keep you alive.

18. A happy marriage can save your life, but getting rid of a troublesome spouse can also.

19. Exercise is key to successful aging.

2

Seven Quotations About Old Age

"It is better to be seventy years young than forty years old."
— Oliver Wendell Holmes, physician, poet, and essayist

"If I'd known I was gonna live this long, I'd have taken better care of myself."
— Eubie Blake, pianist

"Those that desire to write or say anything to me have no time to lose; for time has shaken me by the hand, and death is not far behind."
— John Wesley, preacher

"Although I am ninety-two, my brain is thirty years old."
— Alfred Eisenstaedt, photographer

"Age does not make us childish, as men tell. It merely finds us children still at heart."
— Johann Wolfgang von Goethe, poet

"Will you still need me, will you still feed me, when I'm sixty-four?"
— John Lennon and Paul McCartney, singers

"I woke up this morning and I was still alive, so I'm pretty cheerful."
— Spike Milligan, comedian

3

An Outstanding Read: Growing Old

If you haven't read Norman Lear's *Even This I Get to Experience*, published in October 2014, I strongly suggest you do so—at least review it. Unequivocally, in the opinion of many entertainment critics, Lear is one of America's greatest story tellers. As you may or may not remember, he was the creator of some of the most highly rated, but most controversial, programs in television history. Among the hits were *All in the Family*, *Maude*, *Good Times*, *The Jeffersons*, and *Mary Hartman, Mary Hartman*. Reportedly, at their peak, his sitcoms were viewed by 120 million people a week. Of course, the stories dealt with some of the most troublesome issues of the times—abortion, poverty, prejudice, racism, and the like.

What most inspired me to read Lear's volume was what he wrote in the preface: "In my ninety-plus years, I've tried a multitude of lives. In the course of all these lives, I had a front-row seat at the birth of television; wrote, produced, created, or developed more than a hundred shows; had nine on the air at the same time; founded the 300,000-member liberal advocacy group People For the American Way; was labeled *no. 1 enemy of the American family* by Jerry Falwell; made it onto Richard Nixon's 'Enemies List;' was presented with the National Medal of the Arts by President Clinton; purchased an original copy of the Declaration of Independence and toured it for ten years in all fifty states; blew a fortune in a series of bad investments in failing businesses; and reached a point where I was informed we might even have to sell our home. Having heard that we'd fallen into such dire straits, my son-in-law phoned me and asked how I was feeling. My answer was, 'Terrible, of course,' but then added, 'but I must be crazy, because despite all that's happened, I keep hearing this inner voice saying, *Even this I get to experience.*'"

To help you in your decision making whether to read Lear's book, here are some words of praise from well-known individuals.

PRESIDENT CLINTON

"That Norman Lear can find humor in life's darkest moments is no surprise—it's the reason he's been so successful throughout his more

7

than nine decades on the earth, and why Americans have relied on his wit and wisdom for more than six. It's also why *Even This I Get to Experience* is such a great read."

CARL REINER

"Norman Lear could never write a more dramatic, touching, or funnier tale of his life than he's done here in *Even This I Get to Experience*."

BILL MOYERS

"Many have known the man behind the stories. Now all of us can know the stories behind the man. Archie, Edith, Gloria, and Meathead couldn't have told them better."

ARIANNA HUFFINGTON

"*Even This I Get to Experience* is not just the brilliant, moving story of a man who has lived an amazing number of years—from making it onto Richard Nixon's 'Enemies List' to changing the face of television—but also a life manual on how to live a life of depth, purpose, and meaning."

4

Thoughts About Aging

1. Don't sweat the small stuff.
2. When the going gets tough, the tough get going.
3. Avoid making a mountain out of a mole hill.
4. Certainly, work hard to achieve your objectives, but also remember to work smart in the process.
5. Keep your cool when in a conflict with another person; be thoughtful and understanding before responding.
6. Live in accordance with this rule: never discuss politics and religion with an associate, friend, or loved one.
7. Always try to do the right thing at the right time for the right reason.
8. Do things in accordance with what you probably heard a teacher say to inspire the class when you were in elementary school: "Good, better, best. Never let it rest until the good is better and the better is best."
9. Know when to cut another person some slack when attempting to resolve a dispute.
10. Appreciate the fact that there is little, if anything, either all black or white, since there are many shades of gray.
11. Know that you cannot manage time. All you can do is to manage yourself with respect to how you spend your time (based on your goals and priorities).
12. When a person is talking to you, listen carefully and process in your mind what is being said before you comment on what you heard.
13. Periodically reflect on what you've done, to determine if you could have done things differently to achieve a more effective and efficient outcome.

14. Employ the "investment principle" in your actions. For example, be a volunteer in your community, putting thank yous in your account at the Bank of Goodwill.

15. Listen more and talk less—think about having two ears and one mouth.

16. In all things, keep an open mind without being inappropriately judgmental. Remember, too, in most situations there will be different causes of action to get things done. Accordingly, do your homework in terms of advantages versus disadvantages, costs versus benefits, etc.

17. Accept the fact that sometimes you are indeed your worst enemy. Therefore, listen carefully to what others tell you before dismissing their advice and counsel out of hand.

18. Obvious facts are that we're all human and will make mistakes in life. Nonetheless, everyone should do his or her best to learn from missteps so that the slipups aren't repeated.

19. Just because you are highly educated doesn't mean that you cannot be dumber than dumb in some things. Therefore, be humble. Don't dismiss outright what's said, no matter the source.

20. Demonstrate appropriate demeanor and understanding when a person is telling you something that will make you prone to say, after a few words, something that might be hurtful that you cannot retract and could cause serious damage to your relationship.

5

Book Reviews: Aging

1. *Optimistic Aging: From Midlife to the Good Life, an Action Plan* by Margit Cost Henderson, PhD. I picked Henderson's book to critique because I found it to be captivating, concise, and easy to read. Moreover, I concluded that it could be a useful instrument in planning as one grows older. The work is based on Henderson's extensive research findings about aging.

Although in the introduction there is no table of contents, nor an index at the end, in the closing section, there are detailed notes that show Henderson's noteworthy efforts in developing the volume.

I recommend *Optimistic Aging* to anyone interested in the inevitable effects of getting older, the ideal time to build healthy habits to improve their life, and ways to be at their best as they grow older. A significant strength in *Optimistic Aging* is the recommended reading section. There, the reader will find many excellent tomes on the subject. Overall, on a scale of one to ten, I give it a seven.

2. *The Seniors' Survival Guide: New Tricks for Old Dogs* by Geoff Tibballs. The book's title is what motivated me to examine it. Tibballs, an English writer, is caught up in today's technology and its impact on old people. To that end, in the publication, he discusses LCD, LED, PDA, DAB, FPS, email, iPods, and a host of other off-the-wall topics that are mind-boggling, to say the least. Therefore, anyone with an interest in technological progress over the last fifty years will enjoy this book. Because of that limitation, I give the tome a score of five out of ten.

3. *You're Old, I'm Old . . . Get Used to It!: Twenty Reasons Why Growing Old is Great* by Virginia Ironside. Ironside, an advice columnist for the *Independent* newspaper in London, England, is a novelist and the producer of the one-woman stage show, The Virginia Monologues, first

performed at the Edinburgh Fringe Festival in 2009. Her volume of aging is interesting. My main problem with the work is the credentials of the author as a knowledgeable person to pen the book. That said, I recommend it with an eight out of ten.

6

Effective Communication with Older Adults

I'm a great believer that any tool that chances communication has profound effects in terms of how people can learn from each other, and how they can achieve the kind of freedoms that they're interested in.
—Bill Gates

Two reasons motivated me to write this article. One, May 2016 was Older Americans Month. Two, I'm a freelance scribe who specializes in penning articles with useful information about aging. Furthermore, I'm delighted to have the opportunity to express the following thoughts and views about an important subject to many seniors, based on research.

Several months ago, I went past the eighty-six-mile marker on life's freeway. While traveling, I've learned much about conveying knowledge of and information about growing old, from a multitude of perspectives and sources. Much of it was obtained from being a fighter in the Korean War from 1950–51 and the Vietnam War from 1968–69, then retiring from the Army after serving for thirty years, rising in rank from private to colonel. Subsequently, I started a second career where I worked for the next twenty years as a senior manager in the private and public sectors. Since 2000, I've been an independent author.

According to the Health and Human Services Department (HHSD) website, "Communication changes are commonly reported by older people. In a large survey of more than 12,000 Medicare beneficiaries aged 65 years or more, 42% reported hearing problems, 26% had writing problems, and 7% had problems using the telephone. The severity of communication disabilities is based on a health-disease continuum. Using statistical procedures (sampling weights) to make inferences about the entire Medicare population, more than 16 million Medicare beneficiaries are estimated to experience communication changes. At one end of the spectrum are the well elderly who wish to prevent disabilities communication conditions.

In the middle are the worried well or frail elders who struggle to maintain independent function, and at the other end are people with well-defined communication disabilities such as dysarthria, aphasia, and hearing loss."

In the same online hyperlink, it is stated: "With typical aging, communication skills change subtly, at least in part because of changes in physical health, depression, and cognitive decline. Aging is responsible for physiologic changes in hearing, voice, and speech processes. A person's age can be predicted with fair accuracy by speech characteristics including voice tremor, pitch, speaking rate, loudness, and fluency. Some language skills remain intact, whereas others tend to decline. In the 2008 study of Aging, Demographics, and Memory, the prevalence of dementia in persons older than 71 years is estimated to be 14% of the population, with 3.4 million women and 1 million men affected by the most common form of dementia, Alzheimer's disease."

Unquestionably, communicating with old people can be challenging. Reasons why include: mental or physical ailments; differences in experiences, education, ideals and viewpoints; political affiliation or ideology; religion and so forth. Nonetheless, learning to interact efficiently with seniors can be heartwarming and loving, with many worthwhile benefits.

During the past thirty years, the quality and quantity of communication among Americans has deteriorated. The losses resulted primarily from the use of electronic devices, such as cell phones, computers, fax machines, scanners, and other equipment. Of course, when the age component is included in the discourse, the difficulty is compounded, taking on added dimensions.

Searching the Internet, I found many blogs on communicating effectively with seniors. Here are the best five:

1. Communicating with Older Adults: An Evidence-Based Review of What Really Works (Developed by the Gerontological Society of America), www.geron.org.

2. Guidelines for Effective Communication with Older Adults. International Council on Active Aging, www.icaa.cc.

3. Communicating Better with Older People, www.asha.org/public/speech/development/Communicating-Better-With-Older-People/.

4. Seven Communication Techniques for Talking to Elderly Parents, www.aging care.com/Articles/communication-techniques-to-deal-with elderly-parent.

5.   Tips on Effective Communication with the Elderly,
      www.live   strong.com/article/   149143-tips-on-effective-
      communication-with-the-elderly/.

In closing, I'm reminded of a Tony Robbins' quotation I read
many years ago while working on an aging article: "To effectively
communicate, we must realize that we are all different in the way
we perceive the world, and use this understanding as a guide to our
communication with others."

Best wishes in communicating with older people.

7

Lifelong Learning

Learning is not a product of schooling but the lifelong attempt to acquire it. Life is like riding a bicycle. To keep your balance, you must keep moving. Once you stop, you start dying.
—Albert Einstein, physicist and Nobel laureate

Anyone who stops learning is old, whether at twenty or eighty. Anyone who keeps learning stays young.
—Henry Ford, US industrialist

Happy Greetings! I'm a former Army officer who fought in the Korean War and Vietnam War. Following retirement from the military in 1978, I served as an administrative services manager in the private and public sectors for twenty years. Since 2000, I've been a freelance writer with two books to my credit. As a scribe, my focus is aging.

The fact that I passed the eighty-six-mile marker on life's highway several months ago, coupled with having worked as an administrator at a university for eight years, qualifies me to share these words with you. I was inspired to pen these thoughts, since May is Older Americans Month. It's my contribution in honoring seniors as a charter member of the "over the hill" gang.

According to blogs I read on the Internet, "Life-long learning is the process of keeping your mind, body, and spirit engaged, at any age, by actively pursuing knowledge and experience. Learning and growing helps everyone at every stage of life, and for seniors, the benefits are endless. Research has shown that with opportunities for self-expression and discovery, seniors experience vibrant living, artistic growth, as well as improved mental and physical health. Lifelong learning helps our residents stay connected to their world."[1]

Furthermore, "Whether you loved attending college or university, or wanted to attend but never had the opportunity, seniors should

---

[1]   www.fairviewbenezer.org/Learning

consider the benefits of going back to school. Learning at any age is extremely beneficial for the brain. When you learn something new, your brain grows new cells and builds new connections, which has proven benefits for problem-solving and memory skills. Learning can help improve cognitive ability and memory function and can help ward off Alzheimer's disease and dementia."[2]

In closing, remember that "Lifelong learning can improve your self-esteem and help you live a fuller and more well-rounded life. By continuing to learn after your school days are over, you can develop greater understanding and more breadth of knowledge in the fields that interest you. You can master old hobbies, renew old passions, hone your skills, and improve the richness of your life. By broadening your horizons through lifelong learning, you add to your expertise in a way that bear fruit in every aspect of your life no matter your age, And think of the hit you'll be at a party."[3]

Get involved and participate in activities commemorating Older Americans Month. Every senior deserves, by all means and ways possible, to be honored in May.

---

[2]   www.aplacefor   mom.com/blog.1-11-16-making-education-accessible- to-seniors/

[3]   www.bellevuecollege.edu/ce/lifelong-learning-benefits-body-mind-and career/

8

Mind Deterioration

About six months ago, I became concerned about my memory, having thoughts I was losing it. Occasionally, throughout the day, I would have mind lapses.

My mental situation progressively declined. On occasions, while driving to visit my son, who lived a few miles away from my house, I could not remember the way to go, even though I had visited him many times. Only when my spouse told me that she was becoming concerned about my conduct and behavior did I do anything about the situation—I scheduled an appointment to see a neurologist.

Following an interview with the physician, I met with a technician who asked many questions to determine the state of my mind. Subsequently, I completed a written test. Afterward, the doctor told me that my thinking capacity was mildly impaired and he gave me a prescription. The medication has improved my mental condition. In addition, I've taken the initiative to learn more about how to keep my mind healthy as I grow older. Specifically, I've spent hours searching the Internet for information on mind management. I found a multitude of blogs on the subject. The following were most useful and interesting:

- Staying Healthy As You Age: http://www.helpguide.org
- 10 Ways You Get Smarter as You Get Older: http://www/oprah.com/health/Aging
- How to Keep Your Brain Young (Even as You Grow Old): http://greatergood.berkeley.edu/article/item/
- An interesting narrative on aging can be found at http://www.oprah/health/Aging-Brain-Facts

Lastly, remember, the longer you live, the more vulnerable you become to the growing "old folks spirit." Therefore, continually do everything you can to slow the inevitable process of aging in your life.

PART TWO:
CHRISTIANITY

9

Bible Reading to Be the Best and Most-Effective Christian

Man shall not live on bread alone, but on every word that proceeds
out through the mouth of God.
—Matthew 4:4

There are many ways to be an effective Christian. Nonetheless, the journey has to begin with having the habit of reading the Bible daily. Moreover, to continue the practice until it is no longer possible to do so. Notwithstanding the foregoing, a study conducted in 2014 by the Barna Group, sponsored by the America Bible Society, reported:

1. That skepticism toward the Bible continues to rise. For the first time since tracking began, Bible skepticism is tied with Bible engagement. The number of those who are skeptical or agnostic toward the Bible—who believe that the Bible is "just another book of teachings written by men that contain stories and advice"—has nearly doubled from 10 percent to 19 percent in just three years.

2. While the percentage of Americans who believe the Bible is sacred has fallen in recent years, from 86 percent in 2011 to 79 percent in 2014, it is still a sizable majority of all adults. In general, Americans continue to view the Bible very positively. More than half of Americans (56%) are pro-Bible—meaning they believe the Bible is the actual or inspired word of God, with no errors. Most adults say the Bible encourages forgiveness (91%), generosity (88%) and patience (89%), while discouraging war (62%) and prostitution (82%). Nearly nine in ten household own at least one Bible (88%), and the average number of Bibles per household is 4.7 percent.

3.   Being pro-Bible doesn't necessarily mean Americans use the Bible regularly. Only 37 percent of Americans report reading the Bible once a week or more. Among those who have read scripture in the previous week, not quite six in ten (57%) say they gave a lot of thought to how it might apply to their life. Even as Bible ownership remains strong, readership and engagement are weak.

So, what keeps people from reading the Bible they own? Like all other forms of analog media, the Bible is pushed to the side in part because people are just too busy. Among those who say their Bible reading decreased in the last year, the number one reason was busyness. Forty percent report being too busy with life's responsibilities (job, family, etc.), an increase of seven points from just one year ago. Other factors Americans cite as reasons for less time reading scripture include a significant change in their life (17%), becoming atheist or agnostic (15%), going through a difficult experience that caused them to doubt God (13%), and seeing that reading the Bible made very little difference in someone else's life (8%).

From investigations, the evidence shows the best and most effective Christians are those who read their Bible. Moreover, by individuals who do so as a habit. A habit is doing something unconsciously and often compulsively. Of course, there are several definitions of a habit. An interesting meaning of the word was written by Stephen R. Covey in his best-selling book, *The 7 Habits of Highly Effective People,* published in 1989. Covey said a habit was the intersection of knowledge, skill, and desire. Knowledge being the what to do and why, skill the how to do, and desire the motivation to do. In order to make something a habit, Covey stated ". . . that it was necessary to have all three."

In *Halley's Bible Handbook,* it states, "Everybody ought to read the Bible. It is God's Word. It holds the solution of life. It is the most beautiful story ever told. It is the best guide to human conduct ever known. How can any thoughtful person keep his heart from warming up to Christ, and the Book that tells about Him? Everybody ought to love the Bible."

Nonetheless, Halley adds, "Yet widespread neglect of the Bible . . . is simply appalling. Oh, we talk about the Bible, and defend the Bible, and praise the Bible, and exalt the Bible. But many church members seldom ever look into a Bible. And church leadership generally seems to be making no serious effort to get people to be Bible readers."

Haley's conclusion is that "Bible reading is a basic Christian habit. We do not mean that we should worship the Bible as a fetish, but we do worship the God and the Savior that the Bible tells us about. Nor do we mean that the habit of Bible reading is a virtue;

for it is possible to read Bible without applying its teachings to one's own life; and there are those who read the Bible, and yet are mean and crooked and un-Christian. But they are the exception. As a rule, Bible reading, if done in the right spirit, is a habit out of which all Christian virtues grow the most effective character-forming power known to man."

In a November 3, 2013 *Bibles for America* (BFA) post entitled "Fed by the Word," it is said: "When we read the Bible, we're fed by God's Word and supplied for our Christian life." Also, it mentioned what Jesus said in Matthew 4:4 (see heading above).

Furthermore, in the composition, reference is made in 1 Peter 2:2: "Like newborn babies, crave pure spiritual milk, so that by it you may grow up in your salvation, that you have tasted that the Lord is good." Then in Jeremiah 15:16, it says: "When your words came, I ate them; they were my joy and my heart's delight, for I bear your name, O Lord God Almighty."

Mike Mazzalongo, a Christian minister, in a blog on the Internet entitled *7 Habits of Highly Effective Christians,* wrote: "There are . . . habits that distinguished those who are effective . . . in their personal walk with Jesus as Christians . . ." He went on to say: "I think it is important to have a clear standard to strive for and to measure ourselves against as we serve the cause of Christ in the various roles we have been given by the Spirit."

Unequivocally, there are many actions that Christians can take without thinking. The first and most important thing to do, however, is to peruse God's word every day. With the foregoing thoughts in mind, below are the most important benefits to be obtained from reading the Bible:

1. Provides foundation necessary to know God's will and the teachings of his son, Jesus Christ.

2. Enables obedience to God and reduces sinful behavior through the Holy Spirit.

3. Supplies means to identify erroneous Christians and false prophets.

4. Inspires spending time continually in meditation and prayer with God.

5. Serves as a catalysis for encouragement to cope with difficulties, hard times, and uncertainties in life.

6. Strengthen spiritual discipline via faith in God and Jesus Christ.

7. Brings excitement, fulfillment, and joy in life.

8.   Facilitates mentoring others about God's word and the instructions of Jesus Christ.

Read the Bible! Unequivocally it's the greatest and most useful book ever written. It is the Creator's words and the spiritual foundation for all people who believe in the teachings of Jesus Christ.

10

The Bible and Slavery

To answer the question "Does the Bible condone or endorse slavery," I went to http//www.gotquestions.org/Bible-slavery.html and found the following: "The Bible does not specifically condemn the practice of slavery. It gives instructions on how slaves should be treated." (Deuteronomy 15:12-15; Ephesians 6:9; Colossians 4:1) It does not outlaw slavery altogether. Many see this as the Bible condoning all forms of slavery. What many fail to understand is that slavery in biblical times was very different from the slavery that was practiced in the past few centuries in many parts of the world.

The slavery in the Bible was not based exclusively on race. People were not enslaved because of their nationality or the color of their skin. In biblical times, slavery was based more on economics; it was a matter of social status. People sold themselves as slaves when they could not pay their debts or provide for their families. In New Testament times, sometimes doctors, lawyers, and even politicians were slaves of someone else. Some people actually chose to be slaves, so as to have their needs provided for by their masters.

The slavery of the past few centuries was often based exclusively on skin color. In the United States, many black people were considered slaves because of their nationality; many slave owners truly believed black people to be inferior human beings. The Bible condemns race-based slavery, in that it teaches that all men are created equal by God and made in his image (Genesis 1:27). At the same time, the Old Testament did allow for economic-based slavery and regulated it. The key issue is that the slavery the Bible allowed for in no way resembled the racial slavery that has plagued our world in the past few centuries.

Another crucial point is that the purpose of the Bible is to point the way to salvation, not to reform society. The Bible often approaches issues from the inside out. If a person experiences the love, mercy, and grace of God by receiving his salvation, God will reform his soul, changing the way he thinks and acts. A person who has experienced

God's gift of salvation and freedom from the slavery of sin, as God reforms his soul, will realize that enslaving another human being is wrong. He will see, with Paul, that a slave can be "a brother in the Lord" (Philemon 1:16). A person who has truly experienced God's grace will in turn be gracious towards others. That would be the Bible's prescription for ending slavery.

11

The Seven Best Habits of the Most Effective Christians

Good, Better, Best. Never let it rest until the good is better and the better is best.
—Anonymous

Research documents that every person who professes a belief in the teaching of Jesus Christ should have one paramount goal—to be the best and most effective Christian possible. Toward that objective, studies reveal that the best way to achieve the result is to have a behavior pattern acquired by frequent repetition that shows itself in regularity or increased facility of performance. In other words, to have a habit.

In *Webster's Dictionary*, many definitions of a habit are shown. Doing something unconsciously and often compulsively is the most useful. Notwithstanding that meaning, a more poignant explanation of the term is what Stephen R. Covey wrote in his best-selling book *The 7 Habits of Highly Effective People,* published in 1989. For his purposes, Covey defined "A habit as the intersection of knowledge, skill and desire. Knowledge being the what to do and the why. Skill the how to do and desire the motivation to do." In order to make something a habit, Covey stated that it was necessary to have all three.

Regarding Covey's points, they intrigued me. So much so that I search the Internet to get information about the numeral seven. I learned the number seven is found often in scripture. For example, on the seventh day, God rested and hallowed it. The division of time into weeks of seven days each accounts for many instances of the occurrence of the number. In addition, the number has been called the symbol of perfection and rest in *Smith's Bible Dictionary*. There are at least seven men in the Old Testament who are mentioned as men of God. Furthermore, in the Book of Hebrews, Apostle Paul uses seven titles to refer to Christ. In Matthew 13, Jesus is quoted as giving seven parables. Similarly, in the Book of Revelation there are seven churches, seven angels to the seven churches, and much more, including the number seven linked with God's annual feast days.

Mike Mazzalongo, a Christian preacher, in a blog on the Internet entitled *7 Habits of Highly Effective Christians*, wrote: "There are characteristics and habits that distinguish those who are effective . . . in their personal walk with Jesus as Christians . . ." He adds: "I think it is important to have a clear standard to strive for and to measure ourselves against ourselves as we serve the cause of Christ in the various roles we have being given by the Spirit."

Unequivocally, there are many actions that Christians can take without thinking, but accomplishing the tasks to the highest level of excellence is the daunting challenge. Here are the best seven from studies:

READ THE BIBLE DAILY AND OBEY GOD'S WORD

First and foremost, the requirement to be the best and most effective Christian possible is to know God's word. With information, knowledge, and understanding of scripture, one can be the best witness possible for the Creator and his son. One Christian writer wrote: "Effective Christians are effective because their lives are powered by his Word of God. They know what God says and that knowledge empowers them to make right choices in more consistent ways." To back up his words, the writer quotes Paul's congratulations of Timothy in 2 Timothy 3:15. "Because he knew the Holy Writings from an early age, and this knowledge led him to salvation." The scribe goes on to say that "Timothy's knowledge led to his vocation as an evangelist, as a partner with Paul in missions and as an example of effective Christianity for all future generations."

HAVE AN ACTIVE MEDITATION AND PRAYER LIFE

The best Christians are that way because their lives are powered by the word of God, in the opinion of many Bible scholars. Furthermore, the academicians maintain that they know what God says and that knowledge empowers Christians to keep the Creator's words in their hearts and on their minds. In other words, they are able to stand up for right, give right advice, and say the right thing at the right time, because they know what right is. In support of these statements, these facts should be remembered: Jesus prayed throughout his ministry; John the apostle was in prayer when he had the vision to write the Book of Revelation; Paul prayed constantly for direction; and Lydia was at a prayer meeting when she was converted.

SET SPIRITUAL GOALS

As is true in business, If you don't plan for success, you are planning to fail. To be the best and most effective Christian, set realistic goals, develop and put into practice ways and means to achieve them, and commit yourself to attaining the objectives with help from God through meaningful actions and faith in Christ. Paul saw and heard that Jesus could perform miracles and established the church in the Roman Empire, but he was continually setting new goals to widen his vision for the future and to keep himself spiritually fit.

CULTIVATE THE TALENTS OF OTHERS

Take the time to help another person grow in his or her Christian life. Be a mentor in teaching a friend or loved one to develop and sustain the habit of reading the Bible and applying what's said in the Word to live a holy life. Recall what Solomon says in Proverbs 22:17: "As iron sharpens iron, so one man sharpens another." Apostle Paul expressed it with these words: ". . . we are to grow up in all aspects into Him, who island he the head, even Christ, from whom the whole body, being fitted and held together by that which every joint supplies, according to the proper working of each individual part, causes the growth of the body for the building up of itself in love." (Ephesians 4:15)

TAKE RESPONSIBILITY FOR SOULS

Writings are extensive that the best and most effective Christians are that way because they take responsibility for their own souls and the souls of others. In 2 Corinthians 5:10, it says: "For we must all appear before the judgment seat of Christ, that each one may receive what is due him for the things done while in the body whether good or bad."

SERVE OTHERS

This habit brings to mind what Jesus said in Matthew 20:28: ". . . just as the son of man did not come to be served, but to serve and to give his life as a ransom for many." Further, in Philippians 2:7, Paul stated, ". . . but make himself nothing, taking the very nature of a servant, being made in human likeness."

REMAIN FOCUSED ON THE KINGDOM

This sentence's title is a reminder of the parable of the mustard seed and the yeast found in Matthew 13:23: "But the one who received the seed that fell on good soil is the man who hears the word and understands it. He produces a crop, yielding a hundred, sixty or thirty times what was sown." The bottom line? Know in your heart that the kingdom is forever. It is one of the pillars of Christianity.

By having these seven habits in your life, you will be able to live the best Christian life that you can, no matter what conditions and situations may come your way.

12

Some Thoughts About Marriage from a Man's Viewpoint

Men's perspectives about marriage differ, as in all things. Nonetheless, no matter whether the individuals are Democrats, Republican, Independents, or something else, the following principles about the subject are written in the Bible or come from various writers' understanding of God's words from scriptures:

1. Marriage is a contractual, obligated companionship between a man and a woman.

2. The open relationship is between willing partners, designed by God. As such, it's a gift from our Creator, through his Holy Spirit, that necessitates submission by both to the other. The union doesn't mean, as one writer wrote: "It does not become a doormat. For the wife, it means willingly following up the husband's leadership in Christ. For the husband, it means putting aside his own interests in order to care for his wife. Submission is rarely a problem in homes where both partners have a strong relationship with Christ and where each is concerned for the happiness of the other."[4]

3. This verse of scripture captures the essence of marriage. "This is a profound mystery—but I am talking about Christ and the church. However, each one of you must also love his wife as he loves himself, and wife must respect her husband." (Ephesians 5:32-33 MV)

4. As the old saying goes, "There is a thin line between love and hate." Consequently, in every marriage, no matter its length in tenure or strength, difficulties and problems of one kind or another will surface in actions and words. Therefore,

---

[4] *The Handbook of the Bible Application*, 1992.

always work hard and smart to save the union, rather than leave it in divorce.

5.   Concerning sex, through the joining of a man and woman to become one in God's eyes, it has been said by many writers that "marriage provides God's way to satisfy these natural sexual desires and to strengthen the partners against temptation." Married couples have the responsibility to care for each other; therefore, husbands and wives should not withhold themselves sexually from one another, but should fulfill each other's needs and desires.

13

Forgive and Reconcile While Living

There is more joy in heaven over one sinner who changed his heart and life than over ninety-nine good people who don't need to change.
—Luke 15:6 (NIV)

Men tend to have serious problems forgiving another man for a wrong; furthermore, reconciling with the person later in friendship. As a Christian, that attitude needs an adjustment with a change in behavior. Why? Because forgiveness and reconciliation were pillars of Jesus's ministry. He often demonstrated his willingness to pardon and let pass a misdeed. How? Through love. For example, he forgave Peter for denying he knew Jesus (John 18:15-18, 25-27, 21:15-19), the thief on the cross (Luke 23:39-43), and the people who crucified him (Luke 23:34).

When a Christian person does something evil against you, God's words are: "If your fellow believer sins against you, go and tell him in private what he did wrong. If he listens to you, you have helped that person to be your brother or sister again. But if he refuses to listen, go to him again, and take two people with you. Every case may be proved by two or three witnesses. If he refuses to listen to them, tell the church. If he refuses to listen to the church, then treat him like a person who does not believe in God or like a tax collector." (Matthew 18:15-17)

Remember these words and act on them as appropriate: "Do not be bitter or angry or mad. Never shout angrily or say things to hurt others. Never do anything evil. Be kind and loving to each other; and forgive each other just as God forgave you in Christ." (Ephesians 4:3, 1-32 NIV)

Regarding reconciliation, the term means reestablishing a relationship. Christ has reconciled us to God and to others by his death on the cross. Therefore, no matter the barrier, conflict, or difficulty, this is what a man should do: "All this is from God, who reconciled us

35

to himself through Christ and gave us the ministry of reconciliation: that God was reconciling the world to himself in Christ, not counting men's sins against them. And he has committed to us the message of reconciliation." (2 Corinthians 5:18-19 NIV)

In scriptures, there are many models where Jesus reconciled with others. Among them, the penitent thief; the prodigal son; David, the adulterer; Saul of Tarsus, a murderer of Christians; and Magdalene, the prostitute.

14

God: Building an Everlasting Love

A frequent contributor to Christian periodicals throughout the United States and around the world for over forty years, Wright wrote these words about men who appeared in *The Answer to Happiness, Health, and Fulfillment in Life: The Holy Bible: A Translation for Our Time with Selected Writings by Leading Inspirational Authors* (among them Billy Graham, Robert Schuller, Martin Luther King, Jr., Barbara Johnson, Denis Waitley, Norman Vincent Peale, and many others): "A worthy goal for a man, which may run counter to his early learning, is to become a 'balanced man.'" And that is where Christianity comes in, by eliminating a man's inner conflicts and bringing about this balance as seen in Jesus Christ.

Jesus's personality had several facets, but he did not hide them from anyone. He could chase the corrupters out of his temple in righteous anger, displaying his manhood in what might be called masculine ways, and yet later weep over Jerusalem, displaying what is considered a feminine side. He walked the bloody highways of Palestine, littered with the flotsam of man's inhumanity to man, pursued, harassed, and carrying a price on his head, and yet he could sit and allow a woman to wash his feet and dry them with her hair and rebuke those who thought it inappropriate.

Here is the king of the universe, sweating blood during the deep revulsion he felt in Gethsemane concerning the death that faced him, yet pressing on to take that death on the cross without wilting.

There is no greater picture of the whole man—a man who was masculine in terms of strength, muscle, sinew, and courage, and yet was not ashamed to show his feminine side in terms of tears, compassion, gentleness, and peace.

Related Bible texts about men can be found in Matthew 19:13-15, Mark 11:15-19, Mark 14:3-9, and Luke 19:41-44.

15

Judging Others is Wrong and Evil!

One Sunday several years ago, I visited a church while on vacation. It was an interesting experience and one I will long remember. Among other things were the preacher's antics. While speaking at the lectern, from time to time he would say something profound, then whirl around two or three times. Each time he did it, I held my breath, hoping he wouldn't get too close to the platform's edge and fall about three feet and hurt himself.

Aside from the minister's eye-popping prank, he delivered a powerful message about judging others. While preaching, the pastor took his right hand, pointed it toward the audience, and shouted, "Look at my hand, and remember that when you judge a person and point your finger at the individual, three fingers on your hand are pointed back at you."

I was struck by what the preacher said. So much so, that I reviewed the bulletin I had brought home from church. For the sermon text, Matthew 7:1-5, was listed. I read: "Do not judge, or you too will be judged. For the same way you judge others, you will be judged, and with the measure you use, it will be measured to you. Why do you look at the speck of sawdust in your brother's eye and pay no attention to the plank in your own eye? How can you say to your brother, 'Let me take the speck out of your eye,' when all the time there is a plank in your eye? You hypocrite, first take the plank out of your own eye, and then you will see clearly to remove the speck from your brother's eye."

The next day, after I got home from work, I Googled "Judging Others." Nine blogs were shown. Of those, several were especially interesting. Moreover, particularly useful to me in terms of content and application were:

- https://www.psychologytoday.com/blog/the-addition-connection/201505/why-judging-o
- http://www.allaboutgod.com/judging-others.htm

16

James: The Book in the Bible About the Poster Boy for Men

James, a brother of Jesus, writes a letter in the Bible in which he urges Christians to express their faith in daily living. Men in Christian churches throughout America should read the Book as often as possible. Moreover, while doing so, they should ask themselves whether those in whom they come in contact can see by their actions, behavior, and conduct that they believe in Jesus.

Dictionaries define a poster child as a person or thing that exemplifies or represents. Unequivocally, by its meaning, James is a poster child for how to live as a Christian. In his missive, he writes about fourteen topics of extreme import to men, especially those of color in the United States during these times filled with evil and sin everywhere. The subjects he explores are:

1. Faith and wisdom
2. True riches
3. Temptation is not from God
4. Listening and obeying
5. The true way to worship God
6. Love all people
7. Faith and good works
8. Controlling the things we say
9. True wisdom
10. Give yourselves to God
11. You are not the judge
12. Let God plan your life
13. A warning to the rich
14. Be patient

It is beyond human comprehension for a living black brother, with a mind and blood flowing through his veins, not to be captivated, energized, and inspired to do God's will in his life and the lives of others, by James's eloquent, poignant, and powerful words of wisdom.

17

My Personal Conclusions About Anger

As I have gotten older (and hopefully gained more wisdom, since the latter supposedly comes with longevity), I find myself getting upset often over little things that don't amount to a hill of beans (something my father would tell my mother when they would get in an argument over something that dad didn't think was important). Even my wife, from time to time, would tell me that she was becoming concerned about my behavior. Frequently, after an emotional episode, having said things I later regretted, I would become remorseful and ask myself why I said something so crazy, idiotic, and just plain stupid. As a consequence, one evening I decided not to watch a Monday night NFL football game, and instead picked up my *Men's Devotional Bible* (NIV) for guidance on how to manage my anger.

In Mark 3:5, I read: "{Jesus} looked around at them in anger and deeply distressed at their stubborn hearts, said to the man, 'stretch out your hand.'" He stretched it out, and his hand was completely restored. Thinking about why Jesus did what he did, I concluded he did it to solve the man's human control problem. In other words, as a teaching point for him to get control of himself.

Going further, in Mark 11:15-19, I read: "On reaching Jerusalem, Jesus entered the temple area and began driving out those who were buying and selling there. He overturned the tables of the money changers and benches of those selling doves, and would not allow anyone to carry merchandise through the temple courts. And he taught them, he said, 'Is it not written: My house will be called a house of prayer for all nations but you have made it a den of robbers.'" From what Jesus said, it brought to my mind that there is indeed a place and time for honest disapproval. Likewise, it came to mind that I should learn to show anger in ways without sinning in what I said and the ways I expressed my thoughts.

43

Reviewing several commentaries, I learned that Christians have every right to be upset about evil and injustice. Moreover, they should stand, in appropriate ways, against such evils. The foregoing notwithstanding, it should be noted anger can be dangerous, because it undermines God's love admonition. Accordingly, always keep in mind how important it is to practice self-control of the mind in terms of attitude and expression.

One of the most significant conclusions that has stuck with me is that anger should not lead to sin. Quite the contrary, I ought to direct my wrath toward the proper things to do, according to God's words. Accordingly, I work to age gracefully, with humility, thanking Jesus continually for his death on the cross for my sins.

18

Why Men Stay Away from Church

In an October 29, 2011 article by Thomas G. Long, the question is asked, "What is it with men and church?" In the story, it says: "According to a recent survey, we make up only 39 percent of the worshippers in atypical congregation." This is not just because we die earlier and leave the pews filled with the sturdier gender. The percentages hold across the board, for every age category.

Even when we do show up for worship, we're often not particularly happy about it. This is not breaking news, of course. Study after study has shown that men who name themselves as Christian feel bored, alienated, and disengaged from church. When we drag ourselves to church, researchers say it is not for ourselves, but to fulfill the obligation of our roles as son, husband, father, or pastor.

In Long's narrative, here are the main reason why men are staying away from houses of worship:

1. Men, loaded as they are with testosterone, have a proclivity to impulsiveness, risk-taking, and occasionally violent action—exactly the behavior disallowed in the soft world of worship.

2. Centuries of male control of the church have yielded to an ineluctable force of feminization.

3. Pastel worship, passive and sentimental images of the Christian life, have replaced stronger, more masculine themes.

Bottom line, in Long's essay, since the numbers don't lie, men are staying away from church.

19

Prayer in America

On Thursday, May 5, 2016, people in the United States, by various ways and means, recognized the National Day of Prayer. In a proclamation for the occasion, President Barack Obama said, "In times of steady calm and extraordinary change alike, Americans of all walks of life have long turned to prayer to seek refuge, demonstrate gratitude, and discover peace. Sustaining us through great uncertainty and moments of sorrow, prayer allows us an outlet for introspection, and for expressing our hopes, desires, and fears. It offers strength in the face of hardship, and redemption when we falter."

According to "Statistics on Prayers in the US," Barna research says slightly more than four out of five adults in the nation (84%) claim they had prayed in the past week. *US News* and the Internet site Beliefnet funded a poll to learn more about why, how, when, and where people pray. Here is a summary of the findings:

- 75% were Christians.
- 64% say they pray more than once a day.
- 56% say they most often pray for family members, with 3.3% saying that they pray for strangers.
- A little over 38% say that the most important purpose of prayers is intimacy with God.
- 41% say that their prayers are answered often.
- 1.5% say that their prayers are never answered.
- Over 73% say when their prayers are not answered, the most important reason is because they did not fit God's plan.
- 5% say that they pray most often in a house of worship.
- 79% say that they pray most often at home.
- 67% say that in the past six months, their prayers have related to continually giving thanks to God.

47

A *Newsweek* poll titled "Is God Listening?" indicated that, of those who pray, 87 percent believed that God answers their prayers at least some of the time. Even so, unanswered prayers did not deter them from praying. Eighty-five percent insisted that they could accept God's failure to grant their prayers. Only 13 percent declared they have lost faith because their prayers went unanswered. Eighty-two percent don't turn away from God even when their prayers go unanswered. Fifty-four percent say that when God doesn't answer their prayers, it means its wasn't God's will to answer.

The things people pray for include health, safety, jobs, and even success, valid or not.

Noteworthy is that the Bible contains 375 references to prayer. Twenty percent of Americans forty-five or older who are somewhat religious cite prayer as their most satisfying spiritual or religious experience.

A Pew Research Center survey conducted in 2014, found that 45 percent of Americans— and a majority of Christians (55%)— say they rely a lot on prayer and personal religious reflections when making major life decisions. The same survey found that 63 percent of Christians in the US say praying regularly is an essential part of their Christian identity.[5]

Interestingly, the Bible does not prescribe the time or length of prayer, but it does offer guidelines, according to Donald Bloesch, a scholar and author, written in a narrative on page 919 in the *Men's Devotional Bible*. In Psalm 88, prayer is offered in the early morning (v.13), and in Psalm 55 prayers are said evening, morning, and noon (v.17). The author of Psalm 119 advocates prayer seven times a day (v.164). Daniel knelt for devotions three times a day (Daniel 6:10). Jesus prayed before sunrise (Mark 1:35) and in the evening when the day's work was over (Mark 6:46).

Below are the seven most important benefits of prayer, according to a study published by the Spiritual Science Research Foundation:

1. Improves spiritual life.
2. Enhances the potency of chanting the name of God.
3. Divine help in spiritual practice.
4. Receiving forgiveness for mistakes.
5. Reducing the ego.
6. Protection from demons, devils, negative energies, etc.
7. Increase in faith.

---

[5] http://www.pewforum.org/2016/04/12/religion-in-everyday-life/

Remember that "Jesus frequently prayed for God's will to be done in his life, and we should pray for the same. We pray for God's mercy and forgiveness when we fail to do his will and serve him acceptably. We are to pray without ceasing." (1 Thessalonians 5:17)

Recall, periodically, these things that Jesus said about prayer: "In everything by prayer and supplication, with thanksgiving."

20

Meditation in America

Do not let this Book of the Law depart from your mouth; meditate on it day and night, so that you may be careful to do everything written in it. Then you will be prosperous and successful.
—Joshua 1:8 (NIV)

This is a companion article to "Prayer in America" (*Body of Christ News*, August 2016). Like love and marriage, meditation and prayer have deep-seated connections in the Bible. Regarding meditating, the purpose of the practice is to offer devotion to God, to obtain a profound understanding, and to garner genuine peace and understanding by thinking about the Creator. Many who engage in meditation do so to reach a spiritual presence and union with God. As the psalmist wrote: "Oh, how I love Your Law! It is my meditation all the day . . . I have more understanding than all my teachers, for Your testimonies are my meditation." (Psalm 119:97,99)

In addition to mentioning God's commandments, other psalms refer to meditating on God's work—his miracles and creative power—and his glorious splendor (Psalms 143:5; 145:5). Focusing on our great God helps us keep ourselves in perspective. And God remembers those who reverently meditate on his name—signifying his qualities and characteristics.

Under God's inspiration, the prophet Malachi wrote, "Then those who feared the LORD spoke to one another, and the LORD listened and heard them; so a book of remembrance was written before Him for those who fear the LORD and who meditate on His name." (Malachi 3:16)

The following information about the frequency of Christian meditation in the United States (2014 Pew Forum Research Center's religious landscape study), inspired the writing of this narrative.

- At least once a week: 40%
- Once or twice a month: 8%

51

- Several times a year: 4%
- Seldom/never: 45%

In addition, motivation to pen this writing came from a disturbing blog on Christian meditation written by Michael Bennett, a researcher at the University of Virginia and Harvard University. Bennett said, "Our 21st century is not likely to go down in history as the age of thinking. The age of distraction, of entertainment, of 24/7 technological connectivity, perhaps. But deep thinking? Not much." He added, "Many people would rather inflict pain on themselves than spend 15 minutes with nothing to do but think." Two-thirds of the men and a quarter of the women in the study decided to shock themselves, rather than just sit and think. Most people do not enjoy just thinking, and clearly prefer something else to do (obtained from a report published in the journal *Science*).

Bennett closed by saying, "Yet the Bible encourages a type of deep thinking that is very beneficial in this life—and even more in preparation for the next life. God wants us to meditate—to focus our thoughts on important things for an eternal purpose. He shows us how and why a follower of Christ should learn the art of biblical meditation."

Here is what three well-known Christian leaders have said about meditation:

- Jim Downing, in his powerful book *Meditation:* "God considers meditation a vital exercise of the minds of His children."

- Rick Warren states in one of the best-selling Christian books in modern times, *The Purpose Driven Life*: "Meditation is focused on thinking. It takes serious effort. You select a verse and reflect on it over and over in your mind . . . you know how to worry, you already know how to meditate." Adding, "No other habit can do more to transform your life and make you more like Jesus than daily reflection on Scripture . . . If you look up all the times God speaks about meditation in the Bible, you will amaze at the benefits He has promised to those who take the time to reflect on His Word throughout the day."

- Bruce Demarest says in his tome *Satisfy Your Soul*: "A quiet heart is our best preparation for all this work of God. Meditation refocuses us from ourselves and from the world so that we reflect on God's Word, His nature, His abilities, and

His works . . . So we prayerfully ponder, muse, and 'chew' the words of Scripture . . . The goal is simply to permit the Holy Spirit to activate the life-giving Word of God."

Being fair and balanced, a contemporary phrase in our society, Dr. Paul Meier, a Christian psychiatrist, wrote in his book *Renewing Your Mind in a Secular World*:

> *Man is a totally depraved being, possessing selfish and ultimately self-destructive thought patterns and behavior. Show me a natural man, untaught in God's principles and I'll show you a natural man who suffers from emotional pain. I'll show you a man who is unconsciously fighting and struggling for a sense of significance, using worldly ways (e.g., sexual fantasy, materialism, power struggles, and prestige) in a vain attempt to attain Band-Aids on open flesh wounds, but not ultimate relief from man's inner awareness of his insignificance apart from God.*

Putting aside Meier's views, and expressing the perceptions of people who have investigated the benefits of meditation, the list includes the following:

- Greater health
- Control negative thinking.
- Maintain peace of mind.
- Create the life you want.
- More intimacy with God.
- Increase sensitivity to the Holy Spirit.
- Overcome bad habits and destructive behavior.

Apostle Paul said in Philippians 4:8, fitting words for this article, with respect to helpful things Christians should meditate about, "Finally, brethrens, whatever things are true, whatever things are noble, whatever things are just, whatever things are pure, whatever things are lovely, whatever things are of good report, if there is any virtue and if there is anything praiseworthy-meditate on these things."

Lastly, "Meditation, as described in the Bible, works in conjunction with other spiritual tools like prayer, Bible study and fasting to help strengthen our relationship with God." Too, remember that the Bible doesn't teach meditation that is just stress reduction or for health or peace of mind (though these can be nice side benefits). Biblical meditation is designed to prepare people for action. Consequently, all Christians should think right things so they will do right things. As Jesus Christ said, "For out of the abundance of the heart the mouth speaks. A good man out of the good treasure of his heart brings forth good things, and an evil man out of the evil treasure brings forth evil things." (Matthew 12:34-35)

> *Rappers, pastors, spoken-word poets and authors on Saturday appealed to thousands of evangelicals gathered around the Washington Monument in baking heat to recommit to prayer and hope at a time of intense racial and political polarization and growing secularism.*
> *—Julie Zauzmer and Kirkland An, The Washington Post, Sunday,*
> *July 17, 2016*

SOURCES:

http://www.lifehopeandtruth.com/god/prayer-fasting-andmeditation/
what-is-meditation/Christian/
http://www.bible.org/article/biblical-meditation
http://www.thechristianmeditor.com/benefits-of-christian-meditation
http://www.allaboutgod.com/christianmeditation.htm

21

Christian Testimony

*Therefore, do not be ashamed of the testimony about our Lord, nor of
me his prisoner, but share in suffering for the gospel by the power of
God.*
—*2 Timothy 1:8 (ESV)*

Recently, I came upon a captivating, interesting, and stimulating essay by an anonymous author. The composition was about testifying in church. The writer said, "It doesn't happen much anymore, but in years past, almost every Sunday . . . saw testimony service, which was the congregants chance to sing their own song or tell about some particular thing God had done for them that week, or even ask a prayer request. Testimony service was often the most explosive part of the service."

Later, I went to Wikipedia's website. There it said, "Christians in general use the term 'testify' to mean 'The story of how one became a Christian;' and commonly, it may refer to a specific event in a Christian's life in which they believe God has done something deemed particularly worth sharing. Christians often give their testimony at their own baptism or at evangelistic events. In the current age of the Internet, many Christians have also placed their testimonies on the Internet."

Subsequently, going to Yahoo.com, the following was stated: "Testify means to tell the truth. This is the same as when a witness testifies in a court of law or such. Here the pastor is asking if someone wants to tell the truth of something that has made God real in their lives."

At the gotquestion website (http://www.gotquestions.org), it said, "A Christian testimony is given when Christians relate how we came to know the God of the Bible through the moving of the Holy Spirit in our hearts. Most commonly, we are sharing how we became Christians by God's miraculous intervention and work in our lives through specific events. Often, we can only see that in hindsight, but sharing that experience is vital. A Christian testimony should

55

not end with the conversion experience, but should also include the ways in which the Lord has worked in our lives to sanctify us for His service."

In terms of the value of testimonies in the church, below is one of the best explanations that I read on the Internet, posted by Curve Baptist Church, dated May 3, 2010: "Testimonies make Gospel truth take on flesh and blood. It is one thing to hear a sermon on God's grace, it is quite another to hear a brother or sister speak personally of his or her experience of God's grace. Testimonies invigorate and excite us, as we are reminded that God is alive and at work in our midst. The one giving testimony is obeying the Lord by 'telling out his greatness in the congregation.'"

Finally, all readers interested in learning more about Christian testimony, go to Acts 26:1-29 and Acts 22:1-21. In those scriptures, there are two examples of how Apostle Paul gave his testimony during great pressure when his destiny hung in the balance.

22

Facts Christians Should Know About the Holy Bible

Do your best to present yourself to God as one approved, a workman
who does not need to be ashamed and who correctly handles the
word of truth.
—2 Timothy 2:15 (NIV)

I was amazed, while doing research, when I came upon the following statement on the Internet: "A new study by the American Bible Society showed increasing disbelief that scripture is actually true." Later, to read in a Pew Research Center report that "Black Protestants only answered correctly 13.4 percent of the 32 questions asked about the Holy Bible, compared to 15.8 percent of white mainline Protestants." Consequently, I decided to write this essay. Purpose? To provide readers with information about the subject for their consideration.

Aside from the foregoing, I had thoughts about what I had read in a blog written by Douglas Birdsall, then president of the American Bible Society. Birdsall said, "I see the problem as analogous to obesity in America. We have an awful lot of people who realize they're overweight, but they don't follow a diet." He added, "People realize the Bible has values that would help us in our spiritual health, but they just don't read it."

Bottom line? "There is a biblical literacy problem. Americans, including churchgoers, aren't reading much of any book, including the Good Book," in the words of Ed Stetzer, in an article that appeared in *Christianity Today* magazine entitled "The Epidemic of Bible Illiteracy in Our Churches," dated July 6, 2015.

Notwithstanding the foregoing background, the goal of this discourse is to present ten amazing facts about the Bible that might encourage and inspire readers to nurture a daily Bible reading habit:

1. The Bible was written over 1,600 years ago by forty or more writers.

2. While the Bible is one book, it contains sixty-six smaller volumes. The books of the Old Testament were written before the birth of Jesus Christ. The New Testament covers the life of Christ and beyond.

3. Each of the books, except five, are divided into chapters and verses. The five that aren't divided by chapters are Obadiah, Philemon, 2 John, 3 John, and Jude. The latter are short books, which only have verse divisions. The longest verse in the Bible is Esther 8:9, with ninety words. The shortest verse is John 11:35 with only two words, "Jesus wept."

4. The longest chapter in the Bible is Psalm 119, with 176 verses; the smallest is Psalm 117, with two verses.

5. The Bible is the only tome among various religions that include the actual words of God. The Bible says more than three thousand times "thus sayeth the Lord." And the words that follow are quotes from God.

6. There are historical discoveries regularly found to support the accuracy of the Bible.

7. Research shows that more than 168,000 Bibles are either sold or given away per day in the world.

8. There are no contradictions in the Bible, contrary to what many folks say. Look at the Bible entirely and understand its teachings, which will confirm the fact.

9. Of the thousands of prophecies in the Bible, more than three thousand have been fulfilled either within the Bible itself or since it was written.

10. Apostle Paul wrote at least thirteen books in the Bible. Moreover, he may have been the author of Hebrews. Moses wrote the first five books in the Bible.

An interesting commentary about the Bible is what Dr. Cyrus N. Nelson wrote in the preface of *What the Bible is All About* by Henrietta C. Mears, with a foreword by Billy Graham: "One of the great tragedies . . . is that the Bible is the best-seller year after year, it is not the most read and best understood. Most of us don't need another translation or revision of the Bible; instead we need a rededication and commitment to studying and understanding the one we have."

In closing, I'm reminded of what I read in Henry H. Haley's *Bible Handbook: Revised Edition*: "Booklets for daily devotions, now advertised so abundantly by various denominational publishing houses, may have their place. But they are no substitute for the Bible.

The Bible is God's own words. And no other book can take its place. Every Christian, young and old, should be a faithful reader of the Bible."

SOURCES:

http://www.smallgroup.com
http://www.wnd.com/author/jkovacs/?archives=true;
http://www.pewforum.org/Other-Belief-and-Pracitces/U-S-Religious-Knowledge-Survey.aspx#

23

Bad Habits of Christians

To put off your old self, which belongs to your former manner of life and is corrupt through deceitful desires, and to be renewed in the spirit of your minds, and to put on the new self, created after the likeness of God in true righteousness and holiness.
—Ephesians 4:22-24

Because of media designs, space limitations, and other factors, it wasn't possible to juxtapose what I had penned in a composition about the good habits of the most effective Christians. Consequently, this narrative is a balance to what I wrote about the best things people do that profess a belief in the teaching of Jesus Christ.

Unequivocally, it's very difficult to follow Jesus Christ's teaching as set forth in the Bible. Why? Because it requires you to practice in daily living these attributes: forgiveness, humility, patience, service, and most of all, an abundance of love in a variety of different environments, situations, and the like. Nonetheless, all any Christian can do in life's varied conditions, environments, and situations is his or her best, drawing upon the Holy Spirit.

Researchers have published information in journals and other media about what Christians do frequently, without thinking, that are disagreeable, harmful, and at times unpleasant. Below are some of the most common behaviors:

1. Exhibiting hypocrisy in their behavior and conduct in different situations and interactions with other people.

2. Demonstrating a closed mind, coupled with a disregard for facts, an unwillingness to process other points of view and a lack of empathy.

3. Posting hurtful, derogatory, or mean-spirited information on social media.

4. Making false predictions and prophecies about political matters, current affairs, different phenomena, natural disasters, the Antichrist, and the like.

5. Judging people based on assumptions, false information, hearsay, lies, and so forth.

6. Being hypocritical by actions, behavior, and conduct on various levels.

7. Not listening appropriately and processing information before expressing a point of view.

8. Jumping to conclusions without doing due diligence.

9. Failing to recognize appropriately that being a Christian requires forgiveness, humility, patience, service, and lots of love.

As one unknown writer wrote: "Ultimately, Jesus is what Christianity is all about, not political platforms, doctrinal disagreements, online religious commentary or ominous prophecies."

Concluding, researchers recommend that all Christians should periodically search their minds to determine if they have any bad habits. Further, to read their Bible for scriptures that will give them the wherewithal to replace the unfavorable things in their lives.

24

Let Go and Let God!

Research reveals many African American Christians and churchgoers have heard the popular phrase "Let Go and Let God." Nonetheless, they know little, if anything, about the expression, because it's not in the Bible. In addition, the origin of the saying is unknown. The purpose of this essay is to enlighten readers about the words.

First and foremost, notwithstanding the fact that "Let Go and Let God" is not in scripture, what's stated is based on biblical principles. The following Bible verses support letting go and letting God (all from NKJV):

- Casting all your care upon Him, for He cares for you! (Peter 5:8)

- Be anxious for nothing, but in everything by prayer and supplication, with thanksgiving, let your request be made known to God. (Philippians 4:60

- Let not your heart be troubled; you believe in God and His righteousness, and all these things shall be added to you. (Matthew 6:33)

- Commit your way to the Lord, trust also in Him, and He shall bring it to pass. (Psalm 37:5)

- In all your way to the Lord, trust also in Him, and He shall direct your paths. (Proverbs 3:6)

- Let us hold fast, the confession of our hope without wavering, for He who promised is faithful. {Hebrews 10:23)

Learn more about the poignant sequence of words about letting go by reading Mary L. Kupferle's blog *Let Go! Let God Fill Your Need!* (http://www.unity.org/resources/articles/let-go-let-god-fill-your-need). For additional insights about the subject, read Elizabeth Peale Allen's web exclusive "Learn to Let Go and Let God." Furthermore, especially captivating, informative, and stimulating is Margaret Paul's commentary entitled "How Do I 'Let Go and Let God'?" Paul is a relationship expert, best-selling author, and cocreator of the powerful *Inner bonding Self-Healing Process*, recommended by actress Lindsay Wagner and singer Alanis Morissette, and featured on *Oprah*.

Especially worthwhile to peruse are two blogs by famous preacher and well-known author Rick Warren, written in May 2014: *Let Go, And Know God is in Control*, and *Surrender: Let Go And Let God Work*. The essence of the first is "Every day, you have to decide who's going to be in control of your life—you or God." The theme of the latter is "Surrendering your life means following God's lead without knowing where he's sending you; waiting for God's timing without knowing when it will come; expecting a miracle without knowing how God will provide; and trusting God's purpose without understanding the circumstances."

Warren goes on to say, "You know you're surrendered to God when you rely on God to work things out instead of trying to manipulate others, force your agenda and control the situation. You let go and let God work. You don't have to always be in charge. Instead of trying harder, you trust more."

To obtain an answer to the question "Are we supposed to let go and let God," go to gotquestions.org (http://www.gotqestions.org/let-go-and-let-God.html). Also, a highly recommended resource is the book *No Perfect People Allowed: Creating a Come-as-You-Are Culture in the Church* by John Burke and Logos Bible software.

Make a New Year's resolution to learn more about letting God take over in 2017. Why? Because of what one writer wrote: "You need to do so because it's God's Will."

Jesus prayed, "Father, if you are willing, take this cup from me; yet not my will, but Yours be done." (Luke 22:42).

Make no mistake, your submission, in this writer's humble opinion, will lead to peace and joy, even when the way is difficult. Remember: "Father, I place my life in Your hands!" (Luke 23:46)

25

My Contribution to the Lenten Season 2017

Lent is a Christian season in recognition of the forty weekdays from Ash Wednesday to Easter, observed by many churches as a period of penance and fasting. Below is what I wrote that was published in a beautiful devotional given to members of my church in Denver, Colorado.

Make me to know your ways, O Lord; teach my your paths. Lead me in your truth and teach me, for you are the God of my salvation; for you and I will wait all the day long.
—Psalm 25:4-5

READ GOD'S WORD DAY AND NIGHT

I came to accept Jesus Christ as my Lord and Savior in September 1950. Then, while a seventeen-year-old rifleman fighting in the Korean War, I was wounded. Days later, I was flown to Japan for medical treatment.

While hospitalized in Kobe, an Army chaplain gave me a Bible. From time of receipt until I was released from the hospital to return to Korea to complete my tour of duty, I read God's word day and night. Unequivocally, it became a habit. Also, weeks after I started studying the Bible, I made a pledge to God: If I ever got out of the situation I was in, I would forever, for the rest of my life, do all that I could to live in accord with the teachings of Jesus Christ. To this day, some seven plus decades later, I'm continuing to do my best.

Prayer: God, please continue to favor me with your blessings so that others may see your good work in me as a flawed person saved by the death of your son, Jesus Christ, on the cross for my sins.

Thought for Today: Thankful for his grace and his mercy—grateful.

26

Take Time Spiritually to Examine Yourself!

Recently, I read an interesting essay in *Men's Devotional Bible.* "Examine Your Ways" was the title of the composition. Patrick Morely, a men's Bible-study teacher and author of several Christian books, wrote the piece. What intrigued me were these words in his introduction: "The number one shortcoming of man at the close of the twentieth century (as it has been at the close of every century) is that we lead unexamined lives. Most men have not carefully chiseled their life view by a personal search for truth and obedience to God."

In addition, I may be wrong, but I believe that there might be some body of Christ readers who may not know, or fully appreciate, the requirement to periodically search their souls. Or, more significantly, not understanding the benefits of self-examination or how to do it. The foregoing knowledge inspired me to pen this article. Of course, my purpose is to fill the information void for personal fulfillment. Prayerfully, this will be useful to both brothers and sisters in their walk with Christ.

In the process of creating this narrative, I did due diligence. For example, I read this in 2 Corinthians 13:5: "Examine yourselves to see whether you are in the faith. Test yourselves. Or do you not realize this about yourselves, that Jesus Christ is in you?—unless indeed you fail to meet the test." Later, I went to James 1: 23-25. There I found "For if anyone is a hearer of the word and not a doer, he is like a man who looks intently at his natural face in the mirror. For he looks at himself and goes away and at once forgets what he was like. But the one who considers the perfect law, the law of liberty, and perseveres, being no hearer who forgets but a doer who acts, he will be blessed in his doings."

Make no mistake, in these debilitating, devilish, and turbulent times, we need more than ever before to test ourselves to ensure that we are doing what is prescribed in God's word. Besides, to do it through meditation and prayer inspired by the Holy Spirit. In other words, to apply what Apostle Paul wrote in Galatians 6: 3-4: "For

67

if anyone thinks himself to be something, when he is nothing, he deceives himself. But let each one examine his own work, and then he will have rejoicing in himself alone, and not in another."

Continuing to comment on self-examination, Paul said in I Corinthians 6:19-20: "Or do you not know that your body is the temple of the Holy Spirit, which is in you, which you have from God, and you are not your own."

As an afterthought while reading this, think about what I learned from this quotation from an unnamed source: "When Paul says examine yourself, he is not referring to an out-of-body experience. Yet, it could be likened to that. God wants us to stand to one side and look at ourselves, making an honest evaluation of our progress . . ." No question, self-testing as a Christian isn't easy by any way or means. Nonetheless, it's something that should be done in compliance with Jesus Christ's admonition in John 14:23: "If anyone loves me, he will keep My Word; and My Father will love him, and We will come to him and make Our home with him."

Keeping it simple, just do it.

PART THREE:
HISTORY

27

All of Us Still Need to Celebrate, Learn About African American History

While doing research for a writing project, I came upon President Obama's proclamation for African American History Month in 2013. In that announcement, the president asked the American public to observe and embrace the history and contributions of African Americans in the US. In addition, Obama called upon public officials, educators, librarians, and all the people of the United States to observe the month with appropriate programs, ceremonies, and activities.

Less than two weeks later, to my astonishment, I saw the disturbing, provocative, and startling headline: "Is Black History Month Outdated with Obama's Re-election as President?" The blog was posted by Kevin Fobbs on February 13 in *Civil Rights History News*.

In the opening paragraph of his essay, Fobbs said, "One could make a solid case for calling a halt to the month of February as an official celebration of the achievements of black Americans, since many of the injustices of the past have died away along with the perpetrators."

His conclusion was that there was no further need for Black History Month. In his opinion, it had met its original purposes. Furthermore, his judgment was that black history was mainstreamed into what it always has been—part of America's history.

I strongly disagree with Fobbs. Also, I take serious exception with many others who share his position calling for an end to the historical observance. Make no mistake, I recognize that many of those folks are highly respected and well-meaning, such as Academy Award-winning actor Morgan Freeman. Freeman stated in a 2005 *60 Minutes* interview, that Black History Month was "ridiculous." Besides, he said during the conversation, "I don't want a Black History Month. Black history is American history." Notwithstanding Freeman's thoughts, I submit that a national African American History Month is still relevant. The

71

twenty-eight-day commemoration should continue for years to come
for the following reasons:

1. To provide opportunities for Americans to increase their
    awareness of and knowledge about the outstanding
    achievements and phenomenal contributions of African
    Americans to the United States throughout the nation's
    annals.

2. To afford time for Americans to come together in celebration
    of how far the United States has come in civil rights in
    particular and race relations in general, and gain a clear
    understanding that the US is not there yet. Work remains to
    be done to achieve important national goals for the good of
    all the country's people.

3. To inspire Americans to take actions, individually and
    collectively, to build solidarity, enhance conditions,
    improve attitudes, and upgrade environments that will move
    the United States further ahead, so that National African
    American History Month will truly, in fact and in spirit, no
    longer be required.

At that juncture, as the Negro History Week creator, well-known
black historian Carter G. Woodson, envisioned more than eighty years
ago, the holiday can be eliminated because black history will have
become an integral part of American history. Meanwhile, in February
2014, Americans should get involved and go out and celebrate National
African American History Month.

28

Truman Learned Army Culture Change Isn't Easy

In an army with proud traditions and adherence to proven practices, culture change can be difficult, even when it is the commander in chief pushing the reform. Army leadership is slow, but ultimate acceptance of President Harry Truman's 1948 order to desegregate the military set the stage and pattern for other culture changes, including the continuing integration of women into the ranks and recent acceptance of openly serving gays.

Desegregation took years to accomplish, but by the fall of 1953, 95 percent of black soldiers were serving in integrated units. The last all-black military unit was abolished on September 30, 1954. This happened after years of back-and-forth proposals, in which top Army leaders resisted change.

Kenneth Royall, a retired Army general who was the last US secretary of war and the first secretary of the army, was among those who resisted. "The Army is not an instrument for social evolution," he said in a March 1949 testimony before the President's Committee on Equality of Treatment and Opportunity in the Armed Forces.

"It is not the Army's job either to favor or to impede the social doctrines, no matter how progressive they may be. It is not for us to lead or to lag behind the civilian procession, except to the extent that the national defense is affected," Royall testified. "A total abandonment of—or a substantial and sudden change in—the Army's partial segregation policy would, in my opinion, adversely affect enlistments and reenlistments not only in the South but in many other parts of the country, probably making peacetime selective service necessary. And a change in our policy would adversely affect the morale of many Southern soldiers and other soldiers now serving."

Those concerns didn't stop Truman. His post-World War II decision to end segregation came after distinguished military service by many all-black units and after a precedent-setting move during the

Battle of the Bulge in December 1944, in which black soldiers were allowed to volunteer to join all-white units in combat.

In a civil rights message to Congress in which he opposed lynching, proposed voting rights, and employment reforms, and asked lawmakers to help pass sweeping legislation, Truman said, "During the recent war and in the years since its close, we have made much progress toward equality of opportunity in our armed services without regard to race, color, religion, or national origin." He said he had ". . . instructed the secretary of defense to take steps to have the remaining instances of discrimination eliminated as rapidly as possible."

In 1945, the Board for Utilization of Negro Manpower was appointed, headed by then-Lt. Gen. Alvan C. Gillem Jr. The Gillem Board, as it was called, was tasked with recommending new Army policy for the best use of black soldiers. In its April 1946 report, the panel recommended integrating all-black platoons into all-white battalions, allowing black soldiers into specialty and technical schools, and capping the number of black soldiers at 10 percent, proportional with the ratio of blacks in the US population. The final report said the Army's policy should be to ". . . eliminate, at the earliest practicable moment, any special consideration based on race."

In January 1948, Truman decided to end segregation in the military and federal civilian service by executive order, instead of legislation, and he told the military to start making preparations to ". . . have the remaining instances of discrimination in the armed services eliminated as rapidly as possible," according to a timeline of events prepared by the Truman Library. On July 26, 1948, Truman signed Executive Order 9981, declaring "There shall be equality of treatment and opportunity for all persons in the armed services without regard to race, color, religion or national origin." Truman also urged speed. "This policy shall be put into effect as rapidly as possible, having due regard to the time required to effectuate any necessary changes without impairing efficiency or morale," the order said.

To help make the change happen, he created the seven-member advisory panel, the Committee on Equality of Treatment and Opportunity in the Armed Forces, to work with the services on making the change. It was known as the Fahy Committee for its chairman, former solicitor general and future federal judge Charles Fahy.

This is the panel before which Royall testified that he believed the majority of soldiers would find it "most difficult" to serve under black officers or NCOs. "A change in our policy would adversely affect the morale of many Southern soldiers and other soldiers now serving," Royall said. Royall's reluctance to desegregate the Army drew criticism from those pushing for change. The Committee Against Jim Crow in Military Service and Training singled out Royall for accepting discrimination and continuing segregation as a military necessity. Royall retired in April 1949. Six months later, the Army began moving in the direction of the Fahy Committee's recommendations.

While Royall's career may have ended because of his views about desegregation, another reluctant warrior in the military civil rights movement did better. Army Chief of Staff Gen. Omar N. Bradley also told the Fahy Committee that he did not support full racial integration of the Army. Bradley ended up becoming the first chairman of the Joint Chiefs of Staff and was promoted to general of the Army, a five-star position.

"I personally have no prejudice in this matter, and my only concern is that nothing be done which might adversely affect our ability to carry out our mission," Bradley said. "I would assume that your committee is not only interested in the welfare of our Negro minority but that you are primarily concerned with the need for full utilization of the skills, talents and competence of all our men in order that the Army might be an efficient and representative protector of our nation."

Bradley said he supported "steps" toward integration ". . . as fast as our social customs will permit," but added, "We still have a great divergence in customs in different parts of the country."

Endorsing expanded opportunities for training and promotion but keeping units segregated, Bradley said this would have "several advantages" for the black soldiers. "In the first place, he is competing with men who have, in general, had the same opportunities as to education and development of leadership," Bradley said. It also would ". . . reduce the number and amount of changes from civil life to military life."

Bradley warned that some people would not want to serve in an integrated Army. "We all realize that the donning of a uniform does not change a man's personality, his aptitude or his prejudices," he said. "Complete integration might very seriously affect voluntary enlistments, both Negro and white," he said, and it ". . . might seriously affect morale and thus affect battle efficiency."

After months of discussion, the Fahy Committee rejected the Army's effort to maintain racially segregated units. On January 16, 1950, the Army issued, with the approval of its new secretary, Gordon Gray, Special Regulation No. 600- 629-1, titled *Utilization of Negro Manpower in the Army,* but it still took several years to make the required changes, a plan the committee accepted.

By June 1950, basic training began to be integrated, and black soldiers started getting assignments to units in Korea to fill vacancies resulting from combat casualties in white-only units. By early 1951, all basic training was integrated. In December 1951, the Army ordered integration of all of its units, although it took years to accomplish. In October 1953, the Army announced 95 percent of its black soldiers were serving in integrated units, with a few detachments still segregated.

There was only one black Army general, Benjamin O. Davis Sr., when Truman's desegregation campaign began. Davis, promoted to brigadier general in 1940, retired in July 1948 in a ceremony attended by Truman. Davis was followed by a lot of other firsts. Lt. Della H. Raney was the first black nurse, commissioned as a lieutenant in 1942. In 1972, Mildred C. Kelly became the first black sergeant major. In 1979, Brigadier General Hazel Johnson-Brown became the first black female officer and the first black Army Nurse Corps chief. In 1980, General Vincent K. Brooks, currently the US Army Pacific commanding general, was the first black cadet at the US Military Academy to be named cadet brigade commander, the top-ranking cadet. He also graduated first in his class. In 1982, Gen. Roscoe Robinson Jr., a 1951 West Point graduate, became the first black Army four-star general. In 2001, Gen. Colin L. Powell became the first black chairman of the Joint Chiefs of Staff.

Truman's push to integrate the Army had dramatic results over time. Today, blacks make up about 14 percent of the Army officer corps and 22 percent of the enlisted force. The Army has the highest ratio of minority officers to minority enlisted members of all the services.

PART FOUR:
RELATIONSHIPS

29

Father's Day!

I'm Ben Walton, a guy who is enjoying the best days of his life. Furthermore, I'm delighted to be the author of this essay. In addition, I welcome the opportunity to craft this piece about the third Sunday in June, appointed to acknowledge and praise a special class of men. For the record, I have three children, four grandchildren, and a like number of great-grandkids.

Thursday, June 19, 2016 is Father's Day. This is my contribution to all readers in recognition of this special day in America. Even though I've been a freelance writer for over twenty years, never before have I penned an article about Father's Day. Nonetheless, to do so has been on my bucket list for a long time. Since I've passed the eighty-six-mile marker on life's highway, I've decided to do it now. Among other things, my purpose is to express my admiration, homage, and respect for all men who are dads.

When I began working on this task, I knew nothing about the history of Father's Day. Also, my guess is that there might be others with little, if any, knowledge about the origin of the day designated to pay homage to males who have sired children. To fill the information void, here's what I have learned from research about the subject.

There are several explanations about the first Father's Day. One, an incident that happened on July 5, 1908, when 361 men, mostly fathers with children, were killed in a mine explosion. The tragedy happened in Fairmont, West Virginia. After the incident, Grace Golden Clayton, according to some historical records, spoke to the minister of the local Methodist church, requesting that they hold services to celebrate fathers.

Another other story cited is that the first Father's Day occurred in 1910 in Spokane, Washington, when an event was sponsored by Sonora Smart Dodd. On that occasion, Dodd brought people together to honor her father. At this point in my work, things became interesting.

According to a blog on artmanliness.com (www.artmanliness. com/2018/06/11/a-brief-history-of-fathers-day/), "Sonora's dad was quite a man. William Smart, a veteran of the Civil War, was left a widower when his wife died while giving birth to their sixth child. He went on to raise the six children by himself on their small farm in Washington. To show her appreciation for all the hard work and love Williams gave to her and her siblings, Sonora thought there should be a day to pay homage to him and other dads like him."

She initially suggested June 5th, the anniversary of her father's death, to be designated as the date to celebrate Father's Day, but due to some bad planning, the celebration in Spokane was deferred to the third Sunday in June.

Notwithstanding disagreement on the first Father's Day, Mary Ellen Miller, PhD, said in a June 21, 2015 blog titled *Opinion: Think About Dads Every Day, Not Just on Father's Day*, "Either way, these women sought to have fathers recognized for their dedication to their families in the way that mothers were recognized during Mother's Day festivities dating years earlier." In the same piece, Miller said, "By the 1920s, Father's Day was regularly observed throughout the nation."

In 1966, President Lyndon Johnson declared a presidential proclamation officially making the third Sunday in June Father's Day. Then in 1972, President Richard Nixon made Johnson's proclamation enduring when he signed into law a permanent recognition of Father's Day.

After obtaining facts about the first Father's Day, I turned to what was written in the Bible about fatherhood. I found thirty-four verses of scripture. The top five, based on helpful votes on https://www.openbible.info/topics/fatherhood, were:

1.   Proverbs 20:7 (ESV): "The righteous who walks in his integrity—blessed are his children after him!"

2.   Ephesians 6:4 (ESV): "Fathers, do not provoke your children to anger, but bring them up in the discipline and instruction of the Lord."

3.   Psalm 103:13 (ESV): "As a father shows compassion to his children, so the LORD shows compassion to those who fear him."

4.   Proverbs 4:1-9 (ESV): "Hear, O sons, a father's instruction, and be attentive, that you may gain insight, for I give you good precepts; do not forsake my teaching. When I was a son with my father, tender, the only one in the sight of my mother, he taught me and said to me, 'Let your heart hold fast my words, keep my commandments, and live. Get wisdom, get insights; do not forget, and do not turn away from the words of my mouth . . .'"

5.   Genesis 18:19 (ESV): "For I have chosen him, that he may command his children and his household after him to keep the way of the LORD by doing righteousness and justice, so that the LORD may bring to Abraham what he has promised him."

I read twenty-five essays in the *Men's Devotional Bible* (NIV) about fatherhood. Because of space limitations, it's not possible to list them all. Nonetheless, it would be a disservice not to print some. Therefore, below are the best. It's fitting that I share these with you for inspiration in commemoration of Father's Day. May you be blessed as you read.

"The main reason why a father's task, no less than a mother's, is the toughest job in the world, is that it never ends. The challenges are daily, weekly, monthly, year after year. Being a parent is a full-time job with no reprieve, no time off even for illness and recuperation. In fact, as our children get older, instead of relaxing, or task seemingly intensifies. The point is clear: Once a parent, always a parent."
—D. Bruce Lockerbie, scholar in residence, Stony Brook School

"Every thoughtful father knows that girls, as well as boys, can go terribly far wrong without the right guidance at home, The best counseling services in the finest school facilities have rarely been able to make up for a lack of guidance from a good father and mother who love their children and who tackle the job as a team."
—John E. Crawford, former college professor of psychology

"To any father who really cares about his children, nothing is of greater importance than their training for discipline, their instruction in principles. Together these make up their character, which Aristotle defined as the decision a person makes when the choice is not obvious. My father used to say, "character is the way we act when nobody's looking."
—D. Bruce Lockerbie, scholar in residence, Stony Brook School

If your father is alive, make sure on Sunday, June 19, you appropriately express your admiration, love, and respect for him.

30

Fathers' and Sons' Breakfast

I thank you, Brother King, for that nice introduction.

Good morning, fathers and sons! I'm really happy to be with you this morning. Moreover, it's indeed a beautiful and heartwarming sight to see so many fathers and their sons.

As I look out, I have a vision of the October 1995 Million Man March that took place in Washington, DC, and what that historical gathering was all about with respect to men taking responsibility for their conduct and behaviors, especially toward their wives and children. Unquestionably, fathers have a great responsibility for their sons, and that is to do all things right, that's possible, to make their sons good men. In the final analysis, only fathers can make sons into good men. And we do need many good men.

It's both a pleasure and an honor for me to be here as your guest speaker. And I'm thankful that I was invited. Besides, there are many reasons that I could give for my joy in being with you on this special and wonderful occasion of the Thirty-Ninth Annual Father and Son Breakfast of the Prince Hall Lodges of Colorado. Because of time, I'll limit myself to telling you of two reasons.

One, as a young boy growing up in Waco, Texas, a long time ago, every morning that I walked the two miles to school, I passed a Prince Hall Masonic Lodge, and I often wondered what took place behind the lodge's closed doors—so much so that I said to myself a number of times that when I grew up I was going to be a Mason to find out what was happening in the lodge. Unfortunately, I went into the army before I became old enough to join the Masons and never did find out what was done in the lodge. Therefore, today is the first time in my life that I've been in the company of a large number of Masons, and I'm just excited and thrilled to be here. Who knows, maybe I'll find out something about what happens behind the closed doors of Prince Hall lodges.

The second reason that I'm delighted to be here this morning is because I see my presence as a great personal opportunity to share a few, but brief, thoughts about a subject dear to my heart— namely, father and son relations.

What do I hope to accomplish by what I say to you? Quite simply, to stimulate you—fathers and sons—to think about your relationship. What's more, to get you, as fathers and sons, to make a judgment on whether or not the relationship is as good as it could and ought to be, all things considered. If the relationship isn't what it could be, I hope that something that I say will motivate you to do something about improving the relationship. In this regard, I will point out a few things for consideration in making a father-son relationship better.

What I'm going to say to you comes from a perspective of over forty years of raising two boys and seeing them go through the phases of life, from complete dependency as children, through independence as adults, making their own way in life. As I speak to you, I'll also be talking to myself, because I have three grandsons that I need to do the things that I'm going to encourage you to do.

My subject is TCL—the three essential requirements for an effective father-son relationship. What's my subject? Say it out loud, TCL—the three essential requirements for an effective father-son relationship.

When I was growing up as a boy, the family that adopted me from an orphan home didn't have the modern conveniences that most families in our country have today, like running water, electricity, or an indoor bathroom with a toilet. We got our water from a well in the front yard, light from kerosene lanterns, and we used an outhouse to dispose of our boy waste. Also, we took a bath once a week in a large, galvanized tin tub.

To get water from the well, we had to pour some water in the pump to prime it. I'd like now to prime the pump with you for what I'm going to say during the next fifteen or so minutes. So please stand and repeat after me: "If it's going to be, it's up to me!"

Say it again, but this time, say it like you mean it! "If it's going to be, it's up to me!"

Now, with enthusiasm and passion in your voice, repeat after me, "Good, better, best. Never let it rest until the good is better and the better is best!"

Say it again, "Good, better, best. Never let it rest until the good is better and the better is best!"

Your pump has now been primed. Remember what you just said for the rest of your life, because the simple words have application in everything that you do in life. Please take your seats.

Now, my subject, TCL—the three essential requirements for an effective father-son relationship.

In my remarks I'll say son, singular. If you're a father with more than one son, what I say will also refer to all your sons.

By effective relationship, I mean a father doing the right things to get along well continuously with his son, and vice versa, the son doing the right things to get along well with his father. And I hasten to add, with the father being the role model, example, and leader.

T, the first letter in the three-letter combination, stands for the most precious of all commodities, the most critical of all resources, what most of us never have enough of, but all have all that there is to be had. It's free. Furthermore, it's fair to everyone, no matter who you are or your circumstance—rich or poor, famous or a nobody, black or white, young or old, male or female, in or out of jail. Everyone has exactly the same amount. If you don't use it, you lose it forever. No one can control it. It moves at the same rate constantly. You can't buy, rent, or steal it.

The *T* stands for time!

Time flies!

Time is money!

Time waits for no father or son!

Time is of the essence!

Time marches on!

The first of the three points that I want to make is: fathers spend time with your sons—quality time. Don't waste time. It's too valuable. Life isn't a dress rehearsal. Moreover, tomorrow isn't promised to anyone. Besides, no father or son knows when his journey on this earth will come to an end. Fathers and sons, spend time together while you can, so that you'll have no regrets later because you didn't. How much time? That depends on each person's situation. Nonetheless, it's extremely important for a father to spend quality time with his son.

In this connection, no father should ever say that he can't find the time to spend with his son. My answer to a father who makes such a statement is to tell the father to take a hard look at how he spends his time. It's my opinion that we can, and do, find time to do what we want to do. Consequently, the problem isn't with the father not having enough time to spend with his son. The issue really is that the father has his priorities out of order. Spending time with his son should be given a higher priority. The real key is for a father to set a goal to spend quality time with his son—to make plans to do it, to actually schedule the time to do it, and then to do it as planned.

What does the *T* stand for? Say it aloud! The *T* stands for time, and every father should spend quality time with his son.

C, the second letter in the three-letter combination, stands for what is most crucial to an effective father-son relationship. Nothing else plays such a major role in building and maintaining trust and understanding between a father and his son. It's very complex, because it involves so many things, like personal feelings, upbringing, personalities, education, and so forth. What's more, oftentimes people go out of their way to avoid it for various reasons which make no sense. Without a doubt, it's the underlying cause of most friction and problems among people.

The *C* stands for communication. What does the *C* stand for? Say it aloud! The *C* stands for communication.

By communication, I mean the act of giving or exchanging information, signals, or messages through talking, gestures, body language, or writing.

In the case of talking, true communication between a father and his son should be two-way. Conversations between a father and his son shouldn't be a monologue during which the father does all the talking, never giving his son a chance to talk. Furthermore, not listening to what the son has to say.

I don't mean to suggest that the father shouldn't take the lead in communicating. He should because of his age, maturity, experience, and because he is the father. Nonetheless, a father should give his son the opportunity to speak in conversations, and then pay attention to what his son is saying.

There are many principles and techniques for good communication. I don't have the time here to go into them. Suffice it to say, some things are better left unsaid than said. Additionally, consideration should be given to timing. For example, it may not be appropriate at a particular time and place for a father to say something to his son about a matter. One thing that a father, as well as a son, should keep in mind in talking to each other is to think before saying something. Why? Because there are so many different ways to say the same thing—some good and some bad, some demeaning and hurtful, some uplifting, others a put down. Whatever is said by a father to a son, or a son to a father, should always be said with respect for the other. In this regard, it's said that the tongue is a fire, a world of evil among the parts of the body. What's more, that the tongue can corrupt the whole person. And once something comes out of the mouth, it can't be taken back.

What does the *C* stand for? Say it aloud! The *C* stands for communication.

L, the third and last letter of the three-letter combination, stands for the most important of all human emotions. It's what makes the world go around. It's the greatest of all virtues. In a book that I read quite often, it's described as being patient and kind; it doesn't envy or boast. It's not proud or rude. Besides, it's not self-seeking or easily angered. It keeps no record of wrongs. It's forgiving. It always protects, trusts, and perseveres. From a father and son perspective, it's a deep and tender feeling of affection. It shows itself in devotion, goodwill, and a burning desire to do the right things for and toward each other. In my humble opinion, I strongly believe that it's the solution to all problems between a father and his son. Additionally, I believe that this feeling between a father and his son should never end.

The letter *L* stands for the word spelled L-O-V-E—love. What does the *L* stand for? Say it aloud! The *L* stands for love.

From a father-son viewpoint, love has two aspects. One, the father and son loving themselves first as individuals. Self-love is what I call this aspect. The other aspect is for the father to love his son unconditionally.

Concerning self-love, it will be shown through positive conduct and behaviors. For instance, a father who really loves himself will take care of himself physically, mentally, socially, and spiritually. Said another way, a father who loves himself won't do anything to harm himself, like abuse drugs, get in trouble with the law, or perform an immoral act that could bring discredit or shame on himself and cause his son to lose respect for him.

Regarding the second aspect, unconditional love between a father and his son, where there's genuine there will be a continuing process of loving, hurting, and reconciling on the part of the father for his son. Through the process, love will prevail, no matter what crises, trials, or tribulations that might come up. In this regard, it's love that binds a father to his son, and a son to his father.

What does the *L* stand for? Say it aloud! The *L* stands for love—the solution to all father-son problems.

In closing, TCL—time, communication, and love—are indeed the three essential requirements for an effective, as well as an enduring, father-son relationship. Time should be spent wisely and not wasted in contact between a father and his son. Fathers and sons should talk to one another often. Furthermore, do it with respect and in other ways that are right. Lastly, and most importantly, a father and son should love themselves and each other unconditionally.

This concludes my remarks. I thank you sincerely for your time and attention. Furthermore, I encourage you to leave this place remembering three things:

One: That if it's going to be, it's up to me.

Two: Good, better, best. Never let it rest until the good is better and the better is best.

Three: TCL are the essential requirements for an effective father-son relationship.

31

National Mentoring Month

*For anyone looking to positively impact a community, a
neighborhood, and the lives of your people, volunteering an hour
or two a week as a mentor is arguably one of the most effective and
rewarding ways to make a real difference.*
*—Michael Schirling, former chief of police in Burlington, Vermont,
at the 2016 National Mentoring Month celebration.*

January is National Mentoring Month. The purpose of the thirty-
one-day celebration is to draw attention to the need for more volunteer
mentors to help young people achieve their full potential in life as they
grow.

Inaugurated in 2002, the Harvard School of Public Health,
MENTOR, and the Corporation for National and Community Service,
has spearheaded the movement from the beginning. Furthermore,
every US president since the commemoration started has endorsed the
activity with a proclamation. In addition, participants in past National
Mentoring Months have included leading profit-making businessmen,
nonprofit organizations, state governors, and community leaders at
various levels throughout the country.

A highlight of National Mentoring Month is "Thank You Mentor
Day." During that period, Americans are encouraged to contact their
mentor in their own community, make a financial contribution to a
local mentoring program, or post a tribute on WhoMentoredYou.org
(http://www/whomentoredyou.org).

In his presidential proclamation for National Mentoring Month in
2016, President Obama said this, among other things: "At the heart of
America's promise is the belief that we all do better when everyone
has a fair shot at reaching their dreams. Throughout our nation's
history, Americans of every background have worked to uphold this
ideal, joining together in common purpose to serve as mentors and
lift up our country's youth. During National Mentoring Month, we
honor all those who continuously strive to provide young people with

the resources and support they need and deserve, and we recommit to building a society in which all mentors and mentees can thrive in mutual learning relationships."

Reflecting back, in May 2014, Pamela Laird, professor and chair of history in the College of Liberal Arts and Sciences, was interviewed by the American Association of University Women as part of the organization's celebration of National Mentoring Month. During this exchange, Laird described the implications of mentoring in a networking setting. She said, "Creating a community and network of personal relationships is more valuable than the immediate results of professional networking. The nice thing about mentoring and volunteering is that even if it doesn't have a professional benefit mentoring is doing work that builds community. So it's valuable in itself." Laird received the University of Colorado-Denver Mentor of the Year Award in 2016.

Readers, during January 2017, by whatever ways and means possible, do whatever you can in observance of National Mentoring Month. For help in preparing for the occasion, check out mentoring aids at the Management Mentors website (http://www.mentoringmentors. org).

PART FIVE:
SERVICE

32

Mentoring

Children must be taught how to think, not what to think.
—Margaret Mead, cultural anthropologist

Tell me and I forget, teach me and I may remember, involve me,
and I learn.
—Benjamin Franklin, statesman, scientist, and inventor

Throughout my adult life, I have been a mentor. After joining the US Army in 1948, then later in 1950 as a sergeant leading an infantry squad in the Korean War, I had to do the things under fire that define my mentorship. Subsequently, as a lieutenant colonel commanding a field artillery battalion in the Vietnam War, I tutored subordinate leaders.

Following retirement from the military in 1978 and then starting a second career as a civilian for the next twenty-plus years as an administrative services manager in the private and public sectors, I counseled men and women who worked for me. In all instances, my objective was to help those who were critical to my success as a leader and manager to be the best they could be in terms of getting jobs done efficiently on a consistent basis.

Personally, I didn't take a sincere interest in mentoring loved ones, until my three grandchildren graduated from high school five years ago. When they received college acceptance letters, I said to myself, "Ben, you have got to get serious about giving advice to your daughter's boys." Days later, I developed a plan to learn quickly all I could about effective mentoring. Accordingly, I searched the Internet, talked to family members and friends, attended a one-day seminar on the topic, and read much about the subject in periodicals.

Another thing that inspired me to learn as much as I could about advising was a report issued in 2010 by the National Mentoring Partnership that said, among other things, ". . . nearly 17.6 million young Americans need or want mentoring, but only three million are in formal, high-quality mentoring relationships. Thus, 14.6

million young people still need mentors. That unmet need is called
a 'Mentoring Gap.' As our country continues to move forward with
providing education for our children, it seems that our young black
males are being left behind. This proves that there is a lack of black
male teachers and role models who can service as mentors. There
is a need for more male role models to step up and strengthen the
confidence level for young black males."

Regarding the network, I found these websites to be most
captivating, interesting, and stimulating with much useful information:

1. Effective   Mentoring—www.legacyproject.org/guides/
    mentors.html

2. Benefits of Mentoring—www.3creek.com

3. Mentoring Rationale, Examples, and Our Expertise—www.
    mentors.ca/mentor rationale.html

4. Recruiting Older Mentors—www.connecting-generations.
    org/recruitingolder-mentors

Concerning books, the best three I read, after reviewing eight
tomes, were:

1. Bell, Chip R. and Marshall Goldsmith. *Managers as Mentors:
    Building Partnerships for Learning. San Francisco*: Barrett-
    Koechler Publishers, Inc., 2013.

2. Connellan, Thomas K. *Bringing Out the Best in Others:
    Three Keys for Business Leaders, Educators, Coaches, and
    Parents*. Austin, TX: Bard Press, 2003.

3. Mackay, Harvey B. *Swim with the Sharks without Being
    Eaten Alive: Outsell, Outmanage, Outmotivaate, and
    Outnegotiate Your Competition*. New York: Morrow, 1998.

In closing, if you are an adult with grandchildren, share with them
insights, lessons learned, mistakes made, and the like, to help them
become as successful as possible in the achievement of their goals
in life. Make no mistake, if you do it, the result will be a win-win
outcome for both parties.

33

Volunteerism in America

I have seen Americans making great and sincere sacrifices for the key common good, and a hundred times I have noticed that, when need be, they almost always gave each other faithful support.
—Alexis de Tocqueville, French historian

While researching volunteerism on the Internet, I came upon a captivating, interesting, and useful blog written by Thomas C. Corley, titled *The Pros and Cons of Volunteerism in America*. It was dated May 3, 2002. Corley wrote in the introduction: "The roots of volunteerism in America go back very far. Benjamin Franklin was perhaps one of the most prodigious volunteers in our nation's history, having organized the Philadelphia volunteer fire company, a militia, circulating libraries, public hospitals, mutual insurance companies and agricultural colleges, as well as intellectual societies. Franklin says volunteerism is each citizen's civic duty. Evidently, many agree. Nearly 63 million Americans volunteered more than 8 billion hours in 2010, according to the Corporation of National Community Service, a federal agency that leads President Obama's United We Serve initiative. The value of volunteerism was approximately $173 billion."

In closing his narrative, Corley said: "Today's volunteerism manifests itself in many forms. Parent-teacher organizations, Boy Scouts and Girl Scouts, blood donations, political campaigns, the preservation of historical landmarks, fire companies, emergency services, religious organizations, business organizations and many civic groups all rely on volunteerism for their very survival."

Later, I went on the Volunteer Resource Center's website and found a weblog entitled "Why is Volunteering Important?" The answer to the question was: "Volunteers have an enormous impact on the health and well-being of communities worldwide. Think of all the ways that volunteers make a difference in day-to-day life."

Aside from quotations above, there are a multitude of websites on volunteerism. I found the most interesting site with much useful information about the subject to be www.nationalservice.gov. There

I found these inspiring words: "Perhaps the first and biggest benefit people get from volunteering is the satisfaction of incorporating service into their lives and making a difference in their community and country. The intangible benefits alone, such as pride, satisfaction, and accomplishment, are worthwhile reasons to serve. In addition, when we share our time and talents we:

- Solve Problems
- Strengthen Communities
- Improves Lives
- Connect to Others
- Transform Our Own Lives."

Subsequently, I came up www.helpguide.org. There, I discovered these advantages shown for volunteering:

1. Connects you to others
2. Good for your mind and body
3. Can advance your career
4. Brings fun and fulfillment to your life

Regarding the Corporation for National and Community Service, it should be noted that through its studies, information is available, via reports, on the trends and habits in volunteering across the country, to better understand who is serving in communities, and how, when, and why they serve.

Furthermore, and unequivocally, as one unknown writer penned years ago: "Volunteering, because it is so pervasive, often goes unrecognized. Most Americans probably never contemplate the role of volunteerism in their day-to-day lives and never ask themselves the significant questions about an American tradition. Hopefully, this essay will motivate readers to do so and continue to participate in the activity when and wherever possible."

In closing, I'm reminded of these two quotations:

"Everybody can be great...because anybody can serve. You don't have to have to have a college degree to serve. You don't have to make your subject and verb agree to serve. You only need a heart full of grace, a soul generated by love."

—Dr. Martin Luther King Jr.

"You make a living by what you get, but you make a life by what you give."

—*Winston Churchill*

SOURCES:

http://www.investopedia.com/financial-edge/0512/the-pros-cons-of-volunteerism-in-a
http://www.idealist.org/info/volunteer/why
http://www.nationalservice.gov/serve-your-community/benefits-volunteering
http://www.helpguide.org/Life/volunteer_opportunities_benefits-vounteering.htm

34

Getting Involved

The bottom line profits when employers give workers the chance to help set goals—and responsibility for reaching them. Empowerment, involvement, participation—call it what you will—but the bottom line is this: When employees in a work environment contribute to the group's goals and share responsibility for them, profits go up.

Participation encompasses a person's whole self—mind, body and soul—rather than just the individual's skills.

In his 1988 book *The Human Resources Revolution,* management consultant Dennis Kravetz looked at financial performances of 150 companies in a five-year period, as reported by Standard & Poor's Index. He found that companies with participative management were more profitable than businesses that used an authoritarian approach.

Today, evidence is overwhelming that a company can make more money when its people participate in running the business.

In a recent study of Fortune 1,000 companies, sponsored by the Association for Quality and Participation, research showed that 70 percent of these businesses had some type of employee-participation program. However, the research found that only 13 percent of workers in the organization had been affected significantly by increased profitability and other improvements.

To grow a company and to raise its bottom line continuously, there's a genuine requirement to bring life to business and business to life. Employee participation is one of the best ways. Today, as the twenty-first century looms, the reasons to involve workers in all important matters are compelling. Why? Because most people in the workplace are capable of doing much more than their jobs require or allow. Also, for the most part, they have a strong desire to do more. In a very real sense, employees are untapped resources being wasted.

Employee participation can also:

- Aid workers in exercising responsible self-management in the completion of tasks.

99

- Help people to accept change in an era of rapid, constant transition.
- Increase employee's job satisfaction derived from worthwhile goals that they understand and helped establish.
- What are the secrets to real employee participation?
- Creating an open, honest, nonthreatening work environment.
- Encouraging people to get involved.
- Striking a balance between false participation, which breeds distrust, and too much involvement, which takes up too much time and undermines unity.
- Respecting the right not to participate.
- Allotting time for participation before action is required. In some situations, such as in an emergency, participation may not be appropriate.
- Stopping participation from exceeding the benefits it produces.
- Ensuring that a participant has the wherewithal to get involved—ability, intelligence, knowledge.

35

Grandparents Should Mentor Grandchildren

In these complicated, stressful, and technological times, grandparents should mentor their grandchildren, passing on their wisdom. I came to this conclusion after reflecting on whether I was doing enough to share my knowledge, obtained over eight decades, with my four grandchildren, three boys and a girl, all young adults in college, except one male in the US Army. I decided I needed to do more before the inevitable. Using a football metaphor, I'm in the red zone, third down, fourth quarter, with only seconds left on the game clock.

While preparing to be an effective mentor, I learned these lessons:

- Many parents today have demanding jobs and are participants in numerous activities, with little or no time nor energy left to spend with their children. Consequently, grandparents can get involved and make a positive difference in the lives of their grandchildren, with many benefits for the busy parents, as well as for the neglected daughters and sons.

- Heather Lowrie, a resident of Katy, Texas, and her husband, have three children. Lowrie wrote an interesting article in the winter 2013 edition of *Katy Magazine,* titled "The Importance of Grandparents: Four ways they enrich the lives of their grandchildren." Among other things, she said, "Grandparents have two important luxuries in their relationship with their grandchildren: the luxury of time and experience." When she concluded the commentary, she stated, "Living the life of a grandparent is rewarding because of the unspoken bond that carries on from generation to generation. One day, these grandchildren will grow up and become grandparents themselves, and the cycle of love will continue. They will realize what their grandparents already know—enjoying life, sharing love, and making memories are what being a grandparent is all about."

- Grandparents have a unique connection to grandchildren. The late comic Sam Levinson expressed it on stage when he commented, "The reason grandparents and grandchildren get along so well is because they have a common enemy." Of course, the foe he had reference to were parents. Rhonda Day, a grandparenting examiner and a member of the Virginia Mentoring Partnership (VMP), an independent 501(c)3 organization that helps prepare adults as mentors, said in a January 19, 2010 blog (examiner.com-Grandparents Make Excellent Mentors), "Grandchildren can learn a lot about life by observing adults and mimicking what they see."

- Countless extended family members do not live in the same communities with their relatives. Distant grandparents should not stop sharing their skills, talents, wealth of experience, and just plain wisdom with grandkids because of distance. Rather, they should be creative and resourceful in using modern applications and devices such as email, Skype, texting, cell phones, and regular mail to mentor a granddaughter or grandson.

Aside from the intentional efforts of grandparents in mentoring grandchildren, which provides rewards to both, there's a broader aspect to mentoring in general. Each year since 2002, there has been a campaign held each January to promote youth mentoring by adults in the United States called National Mentoring Month. An exciting highlight of the unified drive is "Thank You Mentor Day." On that occasion, Americans thank and honor their mentors.

In President Obama's 2014 National Mentoring Month's Proclamation, he declared, "In every corner of our nation, mentors push our next generation to shape their ambitions, set a positive course, and achieve their boundless potential. During National Mentoring Month we celebrate everyone who teaches, inspires, and guides young Americans as they reach for their dreams."

Recently, using what I had learned about being a mentor, I resolved to share as much wisdom as I could with my grandchildren.

PART SIX:

QUALITY AND PARTICIPATION

36

Benchmarking Helps
Businesses Improve

There are only two ways to go in business—forward or backward. Standing still is not an option.

No matter how good or financially prosperous a business is, or how good its products or services might be, continuous improvement is an absolute must in today's intensely competitive world.

Benchmarking is a well-tested process to improve a business. Ceridian, L.L. Bean, Eastman Kodak, Hewlett-Packard, Hughes Electronics, Household Finance Corporation, IBM, Xerox, and the US Air Force and Navy are just a few of the hundreds of enterprises that have used the benchmarking process or are continuing to apply it. Benchmarking, however, isn't just for large corporations. Just about any size business can utilize the process.

What is benchmarking? It's a systematic way to identify the best practices, processes, products, or services from other businesses. The goal of the effort is to gain insights that can be adopted to enhance productivity, improve customer service, and increase profits.

During the past twenty years, I've participated in a number of benchmarking projects. Out of my experiences, have come these conclusions:

1. It's a powerful tool that can be employed to make significant improvements in processes, equipment, products, and/or services.

2. The gap between a business's objectives and the results obtained by its best competitors can be identified.

3. It can provide an understanding of what the competition is doing, thus making available valuable information for a business to grown and enhance its bottom line.

4. It compares, projects, and implements. In comparing, it relates the business and its parts with the best organizations.

Moreover, it does so from the perspective of how the best got to be so. Regarding projecting, the business estimates future trends in winning practices and decides how it will react to the developments. As for implementing, the business executes superior tactics and strategies, based on knowledge obtained from other organizations.

5.   To benchmark successfully, as measured by results, a business must take these steps:

- Decide what to benchmark.
- Define what to compare.
- Develop measurements to compare.
- Outline internal sites and external organizations to benchmark.
- Determine the gap between the business's practices and the best practices of other enterprises.
- Create action plans, targets, and evaluation processes.
- Update the process, as appropriate, and do so in a timely manner.

6.   Benchmarking has limitations. It should not be used to:

- Eliminate the need for creativity and innovation.
- Obtain performance numbers from the competition.
- Spy, copy, or catch up.
- Cure all the business's ills.

7.   Benchmarking, like the evolution of the human race through building on others' ideas, is ethical and legal, provided it's done correctly. Simply, the process is an organized method of collecting data from other organizations. Then, after analysis, using the applicable information to improve.

Without benchmarking, a business will never truly know where it stands in comparison to its competition. Likewise, it will never really understand what it can do and how to do it to become the best it can be. In this connection, Sun Tzu, author of *The Art of War,* said it well in the fourth century BC when he wrote, "If you know the enemy and you know yourself, your victory will not stand in doubt."

37

Eight Cases of Lousy Service in a Week Irk Businessman

It happened to me in just one week! What? Eight bad customer service experiences.

1. Having to listen to at least ten rings on the telephone, and then when someone did finally answer, hearing the person say, "Hello, would you hold?" Then silence for three minutes before getting a cold response, "How can I help you?"

2. Waiting an excessive amount of time following a meal at a restaurant, after the dirty dishes were picked up, before receiving the check.

3. Seeing a service advisor engaged in a long conversation with a person who was obviously an old, personal friend, while I stood at the cashier's window, pending the adviser's completion of the paperwork for me to pick up my car that had been serviced.

4. Walking around for at least five to ten minutes in a large hardware store, becoming more and more frustrated in the process, while trying to find a store employee to help me locate an item. And after asking the employee if the store was short-staffed, being told that everyone was in a meeting.

5. Making a suggestion to a customer service representative about how I thought the credit union's automated clearing house payment method could be improved, which would enable me to pay off my loan faster, and being told that I would have to submit my idea in writing for consideration by the board of directors.

6. Going through the checkout line at a supermarket and getting a strong feeling, from her noncommunicative manner and her overall negative attitude in ringing up my items, that the cashier wasn't happy with what she was doing.

7.   Calling the emergency room at a local hospital and hearing the recording: "Please leave your name and telephone number and we'll return you call as soon as we can."

8.   Dialing the telephone number of a government agency and hearing the message to press six different numbers to reach various departments. Then pressing the number instructed and getting the recording: "Please leave your name and phone number."

Clearly, from my perspective, there's a genuine need for all businesses to review their customer service practices. Moreover, to conduct such assessments continuously with the objective to furnish the kind of service that makes a positive and lasting impression on customers, in each and every instance.

My week-long experiences weren't far from the norm for most people in our country, based on the American Customer Satisfaction Index (ACSI). ACSI is a measure of customer satisfaction with the quality of goods and services that are purchased in the United States. First released in October 1994, it was developed to furnish useful information to complement present measures of quality in seven areas of the US economy.

At the close of 1995 (the latest year that results are recorded), the national ACSI score was down 1.1 percent (a decline from 74.5 to 73.7 on the ACSI 100-point scale). In the case of service industries, which includes department stores, discount stores, fast food restaurants and supermarkets, the score was 74.2 percent, compared to the 1994 baseline of 74.4 percent.

I believe that all businesses must "delight" their customers, meaning that services provided must exceed customers' needs and expectations. Besides, as a service provider for over twenty years, I offer these suggestions to create and sustain high-quality customer service:

- Education and training.

- Employment of creative and innovative strategies to learn customers' requirements. Do it, for example, through personal contact (ask questions and listen), follow-up communications like telephone calls and letters, and satisfaction surveys. Ingenuity is necessary, because studies have found that only one in twenty-five dissatisfied customers will tell of their dissatisfaction. The others will merely take their business elsewhere.

- Focus on developing and maintaining long-term customer relationships. What's more, do it via personal interaction. This is critical, because research shows that it costs five times more to attract a new customer than it does to keep one.

- Be reliable and responsive in making and keeping a promise. If for some uncontrollable reason a commitment cannot be kept, inform the customer as to why the pledge wasn't met, and take steps to treat the customer right. And do these things in a timely manner.

- Be courteous, knowledgeable, and provide service with a smile, showing a real caring attitude toward the customer as an individual. Doing this will build trust and reassure the customer about the business's service quality.

It should be remembered that everyone has a customer and each of us is a customer. Therefore, quality customer service is a matter of vital importance to all of us. Accordingly, our conduct should always reflect this reality so that everybody wins.

38

Putting Workers First Can Boost the Bottom Line

All businesses in Colorado and throughout the world are experiencing some level of chaos and turbulence—be they giants like AT&T and Kodak, or places like Joan's Beauty Shop or Sunshine Walk-Up Cleaners. There are many reasons for the current situation, but three come immediately to mind: the rapidity of change, especially in communications and computers; information overload; and people's demands for quality goods and services.

Using the KISS (keep it simple stupid) formula, two things can be said to a businessperson who asks the question, "What do I have to do in these troubled times to stay in business, while still making a reasonable profit?"

EMPLOYEES FIRST

Put your employees foremost in the company. Yes, put people above everything else—computer systems, functional processes, operating procedures, and state-of-the-art equipment. More specifically, employees must be:

- Genuinely cared for and made to feel sincerely appreciated for what they do, as manifested in meaningful ways that are validated through periodic employee opinion surveys and focus group meetings.

- Empowered, after being properly selected for the right position in the organization and receiving appropriate education, training and results-based competency evaluations. In the case of the latter, they should be done on a recurring basis throughout the year.

- Motivated through customized recognitions and rewards to produce a defect-free, quality product in each instance, and/or to delight every customer by exceeding the person's requirements or expectations. Employee motivation should be measured constantly using feedback tools such as satisfaction questionnaires.

Plainly said, when employees believe in their hearts that the business values them above all else, they will be happy, fulfilled and inspired.

Putting employees first results in employees who will do almost anything in the performance of their duties and responsibilities to help their organizations succeed. Federal Express and Nordstrom are just two examples attesting to this fact.

CONCISE PHILOSOPHY

In Federal Express's case, it has a concise corporate philosophy: People-Service-Profit. And the sequence of the three elements is no accident. Managers throughout the organization are taught to first think in terms of their employees. What's more, the Federal Express Manager's Guide says, "Take care of our people. They, in turn, will deliver impeccable service demanded by our customers, who will reward us with the profitability to secure our future." The "people first" management philosophy dates back to the mid-1970s when Fred Smith started the company.

Concerning America's number-one customer service company, a Nordstrom's co-chairman, Bruce. As Nordstrom expressed it best in a 1990 *60 Minutes* feature titled "The Nordstrom Boys," he said, "What distinguishes us from our competition is our array of highly motivated, self-empowered people who have an entrepreneurial spirit, who feel good about themselves, to make more money and to be successful." Nordstrom's people will do virtually everything they can to make sure a shopper leaves the store a totally satisfied customer. And you know what? The company's management is willing to live with the decisions made by its people.

CONTINUOUS IMPROVEMENT

The second thing you must do is pursue a strategy of rapid, continuous improvement. A business's culture should encourage creativity and innovation, with no procedure process or system being sacred—if it ain't broke, break it; thinking outside the box, etc. Besides, everything should be scrutinized and subject to change for the better.

The idea is for employees to look always at what they do, and how they go about getting things down (as well as what is done by their coworkers and others in the workplace), with a view toward improvement. In addition, employees should be empowered to try new approaches to upgrade their own and the business's performance in terms of customer satisfaction, quality, and costs.

Should a given proposal not work, the employee who suggested or tried it should be recognized. Disney and Hewlett-Packard are two large corporations that have capitalized on rapid, continuous improvement for financial success over the years, but the concept will work for companies of any size.

Make no mistake, a business can survive and prosper in these challenging times by putting its people first and using rapid, continuous improvement. Those who haven't tried these strategies should do so.

39

Suggestions for Time-Effective Meetings

Meetings are necessary at times in business and industry to get things organized, to disseminate and exchange information, to solve problems, and to build morale. But make no mistake, they're expensive and can result in much wasted time and money, if not properly planned and effectively conducted. As Edwin C. Bliss states in *Getting Things Done: The ABCs of Time Management,* "There is no greater time-waster than poorly planned, poorly managed meetings."

Those who call meetings can eliminate useless ones and make necessary ones more effective by following some simple guidelines. These guidelines can be separated into three categories—namely, before, during and after the meeting takes place.

Before the Meeting:

- Consider alternatives. Write a letter or send a memo, make a conference call, or use teleconferencing.

- Keep attendees to a minimum. Only those needed should attend.

- Establish purpose. Every meeting should have at least one objective and, if there's more than one goal, a set of priorities.

- Plan details. Select an appropriate time and place. It's wise to schedule meetings back-to-back, before lunch or near the end of the work day.

- Gather necessary information and papers pertaining to the topics to be discussed.

- Prepare an agenda and distribute it well in advance to attendees. List on the agenda the objective(s), topics, and time of starting and ending. If the length of meeting can't be set or predicted, the concluding time shouldn't be given, but it should be made clear that the meeting will end when the objective(s) are accomplished.

- Furnish attendees with background material.
- Prepare a checklist incorporating what's to be accomplished at the meeting.

During the Meeting:

- Start on time. Don't delay starting or waiting for late arrivals.
- Ask someone to serve as timekeeper and minutes' recorder. This should be a nonparticipant, such as a secretary.
- Stick to the agenda.
- Focus on the meeting's objectives and ensure that the goals are achieved.
- Allow people to come and go as their contributions are needed and completed.
- Control interruptions. Permit interruptions for emergency purposes only.
- Summarize conclusions. Be sure that everyone knows precisely what they are supposed to do and when they should have it done.
- End on time.

After the Meeting:

- Expedite the preparation and distribution of the minutes.
- Ensure that progress reports are made and decisions implemented.
- Compare the results with what was specified to be accomplished on the checklist, which was prepared before the meeting.

Avoid meetings if at all possible. Before calling one, ask yourself, "Is this meeting really necessary, or would a phone call or memo serve just as well?"

If a meeting is required, plan it well and conduct it in a thoroughly professional manner.

HOW MUCH DO MEETINGS COST?

When it comes to meetings, it seems that many managers haven't heard that "time is money." If they knew, it stands to reason that they wouldn't squander their time (and money) in unnecessary and/or unproductive get-togethers. These tables, which don't consider lost opportunities, show how much meetings can cost.

One-Hour Meeting

Attendee's Average Hourly Wage	Number of Attendees			
	2	4	6	8
$10	20	40	60	80
$15	30	60	90	120
$20	40	80	120	160
$25	50	100	150	200

Two-Hour Meeting

$10	40	80	120	160
$15	50	120	180	240
$20	80	160	240	320
400	100	200	300	400

Four-Hour Meeting

$10	80	160	240	320
$15	120	240	360	480
$20	160	320	480	640
$25	200	400	600	800

The time spent in meetings take those in attendance away from other activities. Therefore, judge the importance of a meeting and the need for it in terms of cost benefits.

40

Workplace: Managing Your Desk

I had it here just a few minutes ago. J, stay on the line while I look through these papers on my desk."

"Jane, where is that letter from X Corporation?"

"It's somewhere in that pile of papers in your in basket, Mr. M. I put it there three days ago."

"Where is that note I wrote to myself yesterday? I need it for the meeting that's about to start."

Mr. M. has a desk management problem. If his frustrations sound familiar, you may have the problem too.

Research shows that in six hours at a desk, a person spends eight to twelve minutes looking for items and moving things around. What's the cost? An equivalent of one week of work a year, according to John Lee, a time management specialist with over fifteen years of experience who has measured the impact of desk clutter on productivity.

Look around any office. Most likely, you'll see much time being wasted through the disorganization of messy desks. The old saying "A cluttered desk, a cluttered mind" applies to many people.

A person maintains a desk to suit his or her personality, work habits, and the job at hand. Now, keeping a clean desk isn't going to ensure that anyone will get jobs done more efficiently. A tidy desk may even hamper some individuals—but not many. Management consultants and psychologists say that few people do their best at a littered desk. Moreover, they contend most of us could improve our desk management.

Certain guidelines, if used as principles and not as fixed, unbreakable rules, will help you get the most out of your time and effort at your desk.

First, think about your attitude toward your desk and the use you make of it. Do you use it as a tool to get things done better? As a storage bin for clothing, food, or papers? As a display device for family photos and souvenir trinkets? Do you really *need* a desk? Would a small writing table meet your requirements better, thus eliminating the barrier to communication your desk establishes? Is your desk a status

119

or power symbol? By thinking about what your desk is for and how you use it, you may come up with some answers.

For instance, do you:

- Organize your desk so that you don't have to spend time looking for such items as paperclips, a staple remover, ruler, and pencils? Do you place the phone *on* the desk (not on something behind you) and positing an in basket on one corner of the desk and an out basket on the opposite corner?

- Have only the material on top of your desk that is related to the task you're working on at the moment? You can really only work on one thing at a time. Everything else should be organized, filed, and kept out of sight until you need it.

- Finish the task you're working on before moving to an easier or more appealing job? Do tasks based on priorities, one at a time, and avoid interruptions. Stop-and-start-again cycles waste time.

- Use desk drawers only temporarily to store materials; that is, items you need to complete active projects? Inactive papers that must be retained should be in appropriate storage files, not in your desk. And certainly, nothing should be kept in your desk drawers that can be thrown away.

- Take appropriate action on a completed task? When you finish a job, get rid of all the papers, check your task priorities, and move on to the next project in order of importance and urgency.

Here are a few other principles:

- If you need a desk, have the right desk. If you don't need a desk, have it removed.

- Organize your desk before you leave at the end of the work day. This practice will help you get the next day off to a good start.

- Examine your desk management practices periodically (say once a month) to ensure that you're not backsliding and are in fact keeping your desk tidy and organized.

A desk is one of the most abused and misused of tools. Practice good desk management routinely to save time and to increase your personal and professional effectiveness.

41

Time Can't Be Managed: How You Make Use of it Can

What does every businessperson in Colorado have in common with Oprah Winfrey, Bill Gates, Jane Fonda, and Warren Buffet? If your answer is money, you're right. Of course, only from the perspective that "time is money."

Use time wisely and more money can be made. Waste time and money will go down the tubes.

Clearly, from a business point of view, time is the most critical resource. In this sense, each businessperson in Colorado is equal to Oprah, Bill, Jane, and Warren. All are faced with the same paradox: they don't have enough time, yet each one has all the time there is.

Recognizing the importance of efficient time use to success, a number of businesspeople have bought into the time-management strategies of seminar and workshop purveyors. For instance, I recently received in the mail a promotional announcement from a major national management development company with the following lead sentence: "Learn practical techniques for controlling time and making it a manageable resource." Nonsense! Time simply cannot be managed.

My characterization of time-management instruction puts me at odds with a view of world-renown management consultant and best-selling author Peter Drucker. In his classic book, *How to Be an Effective Executive,* Drucker says: "Time is the scarcest resource, and unless it is managed nothing else can be managed." I have no problem with the sentence's first clause. I do, however, take strong exception to the latter.

Time management is more than a misnomer. It's an illusion. Time, fundamentally, is a constant. It moves at the same rate for every human being, regardless of who the person is or how much money, influence, or power that the individual possesses. Consequently, the businessperson's question shouldn't be "How can I take charge of my time clock or control time?" Rather, the query should be "How can I manage myself, with respect to time, so that I can achieve the most gratifying results, consistent with my personal and professional goals?" And I would hasten to add, in keeping with my personality, values and common sense.

In response, I offer these strategies in priority. They have helped me greatly to spend time well, making the right choices of things to do first:

- Audit time use. For thirty days, using a time log, record daily what you do in fifteen-minute segments. Don't be concerned about capturing every activity. Concentrate on the most important events or the ones that take the longest. Record activities as they are done. Upon completion, summarize data collected and analyze the information to uncover time-use problems. It's a good idea to do time audits periodically.

- Get organized. Do this by writing down goals, setting priorities, planning events, scheduling tasks, and evaluating results.

- Eliminate time wasters. Time is wasted when it's spent on something less important when it could be spent on something more important, based on results to be achieved.

If you're a businessperson and you want to be as successful as you can be in these fiercely competitive times, effective self-management, with respect to the clock, is an absolute necessity.

42

Saving Time on the Job a Matter of Sense

Everyone wastes time. But how much time, on the average, do each of us waste on our jobs each day?

At least half of every day, in both white-collar offices and blue-collar factories, according to a recent study by Tarald Kvalseth, an ergonomist and professor of mechanical engineering at the University of Minnesota. About two hours a day, reports Merrill Douglass, noted time management author and founder of the Time Management Center.

Wasted time costs can be staggering. If twenty employees earning an average of six dollars an hour habitually wasted fifteen minutes of each day, one month of wasted time (twenty workdays), it will cost the organization six hundred dollars for nonproductive time—that's an annual total of $7,200. Adding benefits and other costs incurred (about 20 percent), yields a figure of $720 a month or $8,640 a year.

The subjective nature of wasting time is also complicated by things you do that appear to be time wasters, but in fact are time obligations—activities that you do because of a prior agreement or resulting from your role responsibilities. They may or may not be time wasters. The best way to handle them is to either renegotiate the agreement or spend the time to your advantage.

On the other hand, time wasters are activities that you feel take your time unnecessarily or are inappropriate uses of your time. Try to eliminate the wasters, or at the minimum reduce their negative impact on your effectiveness.

Make sure, nonetheless, you're able to distinguish between a time obligation and a time waster.

To come to grips with time wasters, first think about what you're doing in relationship to your objectives. It makes no difference how you spend your time if you have no goals. Wasting time only becomes an issue when you know clearly what you want to accomplish. One well-known time management consultant says, "You're wasting your time whenever you spend it on something less important when it could be spent on something more important instead." Importance is always determined in relation to your objectives.

It's said that defining a problem is half of solving it. Likewise, identifying a time waster is the first step toward eliminating it. By keeping a time log for a typical week, you can tell where your time goes and pinpoint your time obligations and your time wasters. The procedure is simple. Maintain a diary in which every fifteen to thirty minutes you record what you've done. Record your activities as you do them throughout the day. Don't wait until noon or the end of the day to list them. After a week of recording your activities, you'll be have a sufficient number of observations for analysis. Summarize the data, then analyze the information by asking yourself these questions:

- What are the major activities or events that cause me to use my time ineffectively?
- Which of these tasks can be performed by me only?
- What activities can be delegated, better managed, or eliminated?

From your time analysis, you'll likely discover that most of your wasted time resulted from spending too much time on things that were urgent but not important, and on tasks that were neither urgent nor important. The former required immediate action, even though they didn't contribute much to the attainment of your objectives. The latter can best be characterized as busy work.

43

Book Review With a Twist

Best Practices: Building Your Business with Customer-Focus Solutions by Robert Hiebeler, Thomas B. Kelly and Charles Ketteman

Are you interested in how to:

- Obtain and retain customers?
- Reduce operating expenses?
- Create and sustain growth?
- Increase profits?

If your answer is yes, then *Best Practices* is a book that you must read. In a few words, *Best Practices* is about two critical areas: 1) How to meet the requirements and expectations of every customer and still turn health profits, and 2) New ways to approach business problems and how to solve them.

In the book, the three authors, all Arthur Andersen employees, pull together the secrets behind the success of many of today's leading enterprises, such as Nike, Mobil Oil, Ritz-Carlton Hotels, Home Depot, Walt Disney Company, and Holy Cross Hospital, to mention a few.

Factually, in *Best Practices,* the writers outline the creativity and innovations of more than forty companies. In doing so, they focus on how businesses identify customers, survey them for their perceptions of the services and products they offer, and seek to understand their needs.

What's exceptionally good about *Best Practices?* Two things:

- Its organizational structure, particularly the agenda and top ten best practice diagnostic questions found at the end of Chapters 3 through 8.
- The simplicity of the process-based framework that companies can use to meet the needs of both their current and future customers.

What's not so good about *Best Practices*? The lack of graphics to illustrate some of the data described.

A simplified definition of business is people in relationships performing processes. People means human beings with a strong desire to be successful, relationships means key stakeholder relationships (customer, employee, supplier, owner, society), and processes means the steps performed to achieve a desired result.

The book's key instructional point: A company learns how to speak the language of process, build relationships of trust with stakeholders, and is proactive rather than reactive with the forces of change while creating value for both itself and its customers.

Favorite quote from the book: "The search for best practices is about looking outside yourself."

New term learned: Knowledge Space, Arthur Andersen's innovative approach to leverage knowledge for its processionals and clients.

Best practice principles observed in thousands of companies:

1. Constant search for a better way.
2. Development of serious, position, ongoing relationships with key stakeholders.
3. Adoption of a strong "process view" in running the business.

What concrete practical benefit can you expect to get from reading *Best Practices*? The ability to recognize, analyze, and adapt best practice insights. Unquestionably, one's habit of searching for best practices will be significantly strengthened. Additionally, the book is indeed an invaluable quality and participation information resource.

44

Field Artillery Senior Commanders' Conference, 21 October 1976

Good morning, gentlemen.

It is indeed an honor for me to stand before you to discuss briefly what is happening in the Twenty-Fourth Infantry "Victory" Division Artillery. Really, I am delighted to have the opportunity to address such a distinguished group of field artillerymen.

As you know, the Twenty-Fourth Victory Division—the first American unit to fight in World War II and the Korean War—was reactivated on 21 September 1975 at Fort Stewart, Georgia. On that date, I officially assumed command of the DIVARTY.

Presently, my command is stationed at Hunter Army Airfield, which is located on the outskirts of Savannah, Georgia, approximately forty miles from Fort Stewart. The division headquarters and the First and Second Infantry Brigades—the latter just recently organized provisionally—plus certain division troops are situated at Stewart. The division support command, along with all division aviation elements, are co-located with DIVARTY at Hunter.

We are now developing plans to move the DIVARTY headquarters and the 1/13th artillery units from Hunter to Stewart. We expect this move to happen sometime next March or April.

In addition to the organizations, my headquarters is also charged with providing training assistance to Army National Guard affiliated units.

The 1976 missions of the Victory DIVARTY are shown here . . .

My purpose is to acquaint you with DIVARTY's training program—an imaginative, integrated scheme that incorporates the latest field artillery doctrine and techniques and includes the best ideas that we could obtain from a variety of sources. We are extremely proud of our program, and I thought you might find it interesting. I will not, however, tell you anything new that is not being done by most artillery units today.

Being a new command with the requirement to lay a solid foundation of professionalism among our soldiers, the officers and noncommissioned officers in DIVARTY have the unique opportunity to build a combat-ready outfit from the bottom up.

There are ten steps that have either taken place or we plan to take on a continuing basis to attain and sustain the highest possible degree of combat readiness among DIVARTY personnel and units. Specifically, step one centers on enhancing and maintaining the proficiency of the individual soldier. To achieve this end, frequent unannounced individual skill evaluations are conducted through performance-oriented testing. Examples include quarterly gunners' tests, firing battery officer examinations, mechanics' trouble-shooting evaluations, and driver rodeos.

To improve professionalism among officers and noncommissioned officers, step two involves the conduct of leadership-management enrichment workshops. Although we have not met the established goal, our objective is to conduct quarterly one six-hour lead man—that is, leadership-management laboratory for all officers and noncommissioned officers.

Step three is related to step two, in that it aims to upgrade the authority and prestige of noncommissioned officers in the command through what is called NCO Development Days. Each month, we attempt to set aside two days for noncommissioned officers to run DIVARTY entirely, except in areas prohibited by directives. On these days, DIVARTY officers are engaged in other tasks, such as service practices and professional development classes.

To assess proficiency at the cutting edge, we take step four; namely, conducting monthly one or more "quick draw exercises" on an unannounced, no-notice basis. During these exercises, ARTEP tasks, conditions, and standards are used to measure the training readiness of the sections involved.

Physical fitness is essential to the development and maintenance of combat readiness in an outfit. Therefore, we put a great deal of emphasis on conditioning. Step five involves semi-annual physical fitness tests for all officers and men. Additionally, every two weeks, my command sponsors fun runs of one, three, five and/or ten miles. We encourage all DIVARTY troops to participate in the races. To the extent that we can, we try to have DIVARTY Olympics frequently. The Olympics are one-day affairs where troops can participate in a variety of track and field events on a competitive basis. These activities serve not only to better physical fitness, but also to enhance morale and esprit among troops in the command. Of course, three days each week we have organized PT.

Last April, we began looking into ways to improve the functioning of DIVARTY units. Specifically, to upgrade the officer and noncommissioned officer chains of command and better communication between soldiers, especially between the individual soldier and his section leader. Additionally, to improve the manner in which plans and decisions are made and implemented in my and subordinate headquarters, promote better interpersonal relations, and elevate the quality of leadership exercised by junior officers and noncommissioned officers.

Step six is organizational effectiveness activities. These are the results of our efforts. One battalion—the 1/13th—has completed the assessment phase of the four-phase OE process. Last month, I selected 1/13th officers, including all battery commanders, principal staff heads, the unit's command sergeant major, and some other officers to participate in a two-day, team-building seminar. The seminar was conducted under the auspices of a FORSCOM OE staff officer on a resort island about sixty miles from Hunter. The session was considered extremely worthwhile by the participants. Only time, however, will tell the true value of that and similar types of exercises that we shall have in the future.

Monthly, we take step seven; that is a step that I am sure you all take in your command. This move encompasses administration, training, and materiel readiness evaluations patterned somewhat on an annual AGI model.

We are especially proud of step eight, because it focuses on what DIVARTY must do to accomplish its mission on the modern battlefield. We call this the TCA step—think combined arms—series. This series consists of professional development activities for all combat arms officers in the division. Fire support planning and coordination workshops, service practices using the DIVARTY 14.5 range, and classes on subjects covered in Training Circular 6-100—combined arms team effectiveness—are kinds of events included in TCA.

Close look drills, which is step nine on our stepladder, leading to combat readiness, involves quarterly battery ARTEP assessments and battalion ARTEP evaluations on a semi-annual basis.

Lastly, gentlemen, is step ten—that is, quarterly tactical DIVARTY command post exercises, which we refer to as tactical shakedowns. The main objective of these exercises is to keep my headquarters operationally proficient and capable of accomplishing its tactical mission in a simulated battlefield environment. We plan to have a tactical shakedown early next month, during which we will have our first opportunity to evaluate the field artillery counterfire concept using the typical DIVARTY tactical operations center set forth in Training Circular 6-20-4.

In the weeks and months ahead, as my command grows, these ten steps will be taken. Over and over again as the situation warrants, in order to develop and maintain the best possible degree of combat readiness.

Fellow REDLEGS, this concludes my presentation. I would be happy to answer any questions you might have about anything that I have covered, or about the Victory DIVARTY in general.

PART SEVEN:
SELF-HELP

45

Benefits of Meditation

In 2016, I wrote several articles, which were published in periodicals, about meditation. Recently, while doing research, I came upon an interesting blog at www. more.com about the subject, dated November 2013, titled *The Anti-Aging Benefits of Meditation*. I found the piece to be captivating, interesting, and stimulating. Most striking, however, was the extensive documentation cited in the writing that clearly established pondering's health advantages as a person grows older. Because the 50 Plus Marketplace is the information resources for people fifty years and older, I thought it might be worthwhile to share the work with readers. Accordingly, the entire composition is quoted below, in keeping with one of the publication's January themes, namely, health and fitness.

Does meditation turn back your biological clock? A number of studies suggest the answer is yes. For instance, a study published this year found that people who meditated daily for at least four years had longer telomeres—the protective caps on the ends of chromosomes-than people who do not meditate. Short telomeres are believed to be markers of accelerated aging, according to the study's lead author, Elizabeth A Hoge, MD, assistant professor of psychiatry at Harvard Medical School.

Scientists have also shown that meditation may reverse the effects of aging on the brain. As we grow older, the prefrontal cortex-region of the brain associated with attention and planning-gets thinner. In 2005, Sara Lazar, PhD, also with Harvard's psychiatry department, found that meditators had thicker prefrontal cortexes than did nonmeditators.

Similarly, in 2010, scientists at the University of Pennsylvania discovered that, compared with nonmeditators, meditators have significantly greater blood flow in their brains-a sign of robust brain activity. The same group also found that training people who have signs of memory decline to meditate increased their cerebral blood flow and memory. "We believe that doing meditation improves your memory and attention in the long run," says Andrew Newberg, MD, the senior author of both studies and now Director of Research at Thomas Jefferson University Hospital.

Several different types of meditation produce anti-aging benefits. Participants in Hoge's study did "loving kindness" meditation. This sometimes involves ". . . repeating a series of phrases that you direct toward another person, like 'May you be well,' 'May you be healthy,' 'May you be at ease,'" Hoge explains. The University of Pennsylvania group engaged in Kirtan Kriya, a singing meditation.

Hoge says: "Meditation may keep you young because it decreases the body's production of stress hormones, which have negative effects, such as tissue damage. In particular, loving-kindness meditation may be valuable because it guides practitioners to think of other people—a social focus that may increase the activity of oxytocin in the brain, a hormone whose levels can increase when you hug someone. Boosts in oxytocin have been linked to health benefits, such as lower blood pressure and faster wound healing.

46

Contentment

Be thankful for what you have; you'll end up having more. If you concentrate on what you don't have, you will never, ever have enough!
—Oprah Winfrey

While reading the February 27–March 6, 2017 issue of *Time*, I came upon an interesting article in "The View, How to Make Life Easier" section titled, "Success—How to Create More from What You Already Have" by Scott Sonenshein. Sonenshein, a professor of management at Rice University and author of *Stretch: Unlock the Power of Less and Achieve More Than You Ever Imagined,* captivated me in his opening statement. He wrote, "Ask most people to describe the path to success and their answer will likely call for 'more'—more money to buy things, more time to do things and more knowledge to inform things. There's an intuitive appeal to this argument. In terms of success, more is the thought to be a cause (the more we have, the more we can do) and a consequence (to the victor go the spoils)."

In closing, Sonenshein wrote, "You already have everything you need to succeed. Just stretch. Imagine how liberating it would be to stop worrying about what you don't have and start engaging with what you already do have in more productive and satisfying ways."

Coincidentally, while doing research, I picked up a copy of the January 2017 edition of *Guidepost* where, to my surprise, I came upon this interesting and related quote by Pharrell Williams, who produced and composed the music for the inspirational movie, *Hidden Figures.* "Of course, it's not possible to experience constant euphoria, but if you're grateful, you can find happiness in everything."

Also, I would be remiss if I didn't report what one of the most admired motivators, Dale Carnegie, said many years ago about contentment: "It isn't what you have or what you are doing that makes you happy or unhappy. It is what you think about it." Then, to add fuel to the fire, the compelling words of Pearl S. Buck, the famous novelist who was awarded the 1938 Nobel Prize in literature. "Many people lose the small joys in the hope for the big happiness."

Of course, I would be negligent if I didn't add a spiritual dimension to this commentary. Therefore, my thoughts race to what is said in the Holy Bible. Two verses of scripture are especially applicable. First, Matthew 6:24: "No one can serve two masters. Either he will hate the one and love the other, or he will be devoted to the one and despise the other. You cannot serve both God and money." Two, Philippians 4:12: "I know what it is to have plenty. I have learned the secret of being content in any and every situation, whether well fed or hungry. Whether living in plenty or in want."

Regarding the secret of spiritual contentment, I strongly recommend a blog dated May 29, 2014, written by Sam Storms. Also, it would be worth the time to read what Pastor Rick Warden wrote in a September 26, 2016 weblog entitled "Contentment is a Sign of Spiritual Maturity."

In closing, make no mistake, everyone needs to learn contentment, because, as is said in Ecclesiastes 6:9, "It is better to be satisfied with what you have than to be always wanting something else."

47

Everyone Should Resolve to Practice Empathy in 2017

Never criticize a man until you've walked a mile in his moccasins.
—American Indian proverb

As a freelance scribe, my calling is to write articles about subjects that relate harmoniously with readers. In other words, to pen literary compositions that are useful to readers in meaningful ways. Toward that end, I was moved to create this narrative based on what President Barrack Obama said in 2006 about empathy: "I think we should talk more about our empathy deficit—the ability to put ourselves in someone else's shoes; to see the world through the eyes of those who are different from us—the child who's hungry, the steelworkers who's been laid off, the family who lost the entire life they built together when the storm came to town. When you think like this, when you choose to broaden your ambit of concern and empathize with the plight of others, whether they are close friends or distant strangers, it becomes harder not to act, harder not to help."

Aside from President Obama's inspiration, a post on Greater Good's website, written by Roman Krznaric, PhD, author of *Empathy: Why it Matters and How to Get It*, also motivated me to pen this essay. In his blog, Krznaric wrote, "If you think you're hearing the word 'empathy' everywhere, you're right. It's now on the lips of scientists and business leaders, education experts, and political activists. But there is a vital question that few people ask: How can I expand my own empathic potential? Empathy is not just a way to extend the boundaries of your moral universe. Per new research, it's a habit we can cultivate to improve the quality of our own lives."

Answering the obvious question, what is empathy? Krznaric wrote, "It's the ability to step into the shoes of another person, aiming to understand their feelings and perspective, and to use that understanding to guide our actions. That makes it different from kindness or pity. And

137

don't confuse it with the Golden Rule—Do unto others as you would have them do unto you—they might have different tastes." Empathy is about discovering those tastes.

Interestingly, Daniel Goleman, author of *Emotional Intelligence*, says, ". . . empathy is basically the ability to understand others' emotions." He also said, however, that ". . . at a deeper level it is about defining, understanding, and reacting to the concerns and needs that underlie others' emotional responses and reactions."

Make no mistake, be under no illusions, in these difficult and turbulent days in the United States, there's a requirement for everyone to be empathetic in their daily living. Go to these websites to learn more about empathy:

1.   http://www.   improveyoursocialskills.com/empathy/ understanding-yourself

2.   http://www.   improveyoursocialskills.com/empathy/ understanding-others

3.   http://www.   improveyoursocialskills.com/empathy/ nonverbal-empathy.

Remember that the knowledge you obtain from learning the essentials of empathy can help you immediately in understanding what someone else is thinking or feeling, resulting in making it easier for you to interact more effectively with the person.

48

Get More Out of Your Time and Life: Kick the Worry Habit

What does procrastination have in common with worry? Both are time-killing emotions that come from habit—a bad habit. In addition, because of their psychological base, both can be debilitating. At worst, worry can kill you. As any good doctor will tell you: "You do not get stomach ulcers from what you eat. You get ulcers from what is eating you."

In this regard, it's fitting to paraphrase the admonition given to businessmen some years ago, by Dr. Alex Carrel, world-famous Franco-American surgeon and biologist: People who do not know how to fight worry die young. And, as Robert Lee Frost said, "The reason worry kills more people than work is that more people worry than work."

Dr. John A. Schindler writes in his best-selling book *How to Live 365 Days a Year* (Fawcett Publications, 1968) that "It's the worried man in industry who has most of the accidents. Attention to the job is interrupted by a train of thought about a disagreeable problem—possibly trouble with the wife at home—possibly trouble over the house mortgage—possibly anxiety over a dozen things—then zingo! Zip! He loses his hand in a press or a moving rod pierces his arm. Seventy-five percent of the accidents happen to repeaters." And, I hasten to add, women too can experience the same thing in industry (or in the kitchen at home) from worry.

When you worry, you feel uneasy about some uncertain or threatening matter. By definition, worry is future oriented. Nothing that we worry about exists in the present, and most won't exist in the future either, which brings to mind what Mark Twain once remarked: "I've suffered a great many catastrophes in my life. Most of them never happened."

The reality is that only you can worry. Moreover, nobody can make you worry. Since we are humans, we all worry about something at some time or another. Unfortunately, as expectations of what we want to get out of our time and life (material possessions, financial security, success, and the like) grows, coupled with: 1) the ever constant, rapid rate of technological change, which we're experiencing each year, and 2) the increasing complexity of just living and making ends meet, we are now worrying more and more. In the course of our worrying, we waste valuable time—time that we could put to better use in pursuit of our personal and professional goals.

What do we worry about? How we look, growing old, hurting someone's feelings, money, being accepted, not being respected, job security, children, health and on and on—the list of potential worries is endless. In this regard, it's interesting to note that a recent study found that 40 percent of what people worry about, never happened, 35 percent couldn't be changed, 15 percent turned to better than expected, 8 percent were petty, useless worries, and only 2 percent could even be remotely labeled as legitimate worries.

Do you waste time worrying about things? If you do, here are some ideas and techniques that can help you kick the habit, make you feel better about yourself, and enable you to get more things done in less time.

- Determine as precisely as you can what's troubling you when you begin to worry about something. Ask yourself, "What's the worst that could happen?" Write it down and assign a rating to it on a scale of one to ten. Base your rating on: 1) its potential adverse impact on you, your family, friend, or whatever, and 2) the likelihood that it will happen. Then take appropriate steps to reduce the chances of what might happen from occurring. Prepare yourself mentally, however, to accept the worst, if necessary. In this connection, say to yourself familiar prayer of serenity:

God grant me the serenity
To accept the things I cannot change;
The courage to change the things I can;
And the wisdom to know the difference.

or, if the prayer bothers you, say the old Mother Goose nursery rhyme:

For every ailment under the sun,
There is a remedy, or there is none;
If there be one, try to find it;
If there be none, never mind it.

- When you are faced with a problem or negative thought, take the time right then and there (or as soon as possible thereafter) to think it through. Analyze the matter mentally. Gather as any facts and other information as you can about the difficulty. Talk to other folks about the problem, if that's appropriate. Summarize everything on paper. Weigh the pros and cons of what you've collected and bite the bullet— decide what you're going to do and do it. Don't procrastinate. If you make the wrong judgment, so be it. Don't waste time and energy fretting over what's done. Chalk it up as a learning experience and move on to something else.

- Prevent worry from entering your mind by staying busy doing constructive and positive things. Get involved in some type of activity that will permit you to spend your time productively.

- Never fight a problem. Learn to cooperate with what can't be changed. Tell yourself, "This is so. I cannot do anything about it. Therefore, I'm not going to let it worry me, period." The use of the law of averages can help you get rid of worries too. For example, think back over the past year of your life and put on paper all the significant things you worried about. Put a checkmark by each that never came to pass and a dot by any that turned out to be a blessing in disguise. See what's left. Figure out the odds: worrying vs. not worrying about things.

- Make sure your goals are clear, specific, and not in conflict with each other. Always have a purpose for what you do. Frequently look at where you are in relation to what you're trying to accomplish in the time you have available. Use some type of plan to guide you toward your goals, and do things to achieve them in a balanced, sensible, and systematic way.

- Do things in order of their importance. Operate on the basis of priorities. Accept the fact up front that you (or anyone else, for that matter) can't do everything you would like; there isn't enough time. Choices, from among many alternatives, have to be made.

- Schedule time to worry, say fifteen to thirty minutes, once a week or daily (if you have a real bad habit). During these periods, which should be the same weekly or daily, do nothing but worry. Progressively, however, shorten the time you spend worrying, until you lick the affliction or bring it under acceptable control.

- Maintain a worry list. Write down all the things that might go wrong that bothers you. Keep the list up to date. When the mood hits you, look the list over and note what has actually happened to the things you wrote. Base your worrying on what you learn from your list reviews.

Time, the most precious and scarcest of all resources—a resource that has an impact on every single thing that everybody does—should not be wasted by a person worrying about something. Put worry in its place. Keep it away from you or, barring that, control it. You'll be happier with less stress and tension in your life if you do. Additionally, you'll have time to do other, more profitable, things. Yes, you may also live longer (than you would otherwise).

Get more out of your time and life: kick the worry habit once and for all. You can do it if you try!

49

How to Fight Procrastination and Win

Procrastination! What is it? Deferring, postponing, or putting off doing something that you know you should be doing or that you know you must do. Said another way, procrastination is doing something that pays off little in terms of what you get in return for the time you devote to the action, when you could or should be spending that time on a higher-payoff task. For example, watching television when you should be working on something in the house; reading the newspaper instead of preparing a report; or avoiding a person, rather than telling the individual the bad news. Procrastination is also playing the "I'm gonna" game—I'm gonna invest my money next year; I'm gonna spend more time with my family when I get this project at work completed; I'm gonna talk to my son about his problem soon; I'm gonna get that physical checkup the first chance I get; I'm gonna take a vacation when I get more money saved; and on and on.

Who procrastinates? Guess? You're right! We all do to some degree. It's a universal human condition. And all procrastination isn't bad. Sometimes delaying or postponing an action is the best thing to do. Certainly, as the adage goes, "haste does make waste." Procrastination is a problem for you, however, when you neglect or put off doing important things that will help you accomplish what you should or must do, and do instead things that have little or no bearing on your personal or professional goals. In the latter instances, procrastination is definitely your enemy. And it can be a tough opponent. You must fight it!

What causes you to procrastinate? Mainly habit, followed by fear. We all like to do things that are easy and enjoyable. Seldom do we put off doing something that makes us feel good. On the other hand, most people are slow or never get around to doing something that is either unpleasant, difficult, or that requires a tough decision be made. As for fear, being afraid of either making a mistake, offending a person, or being too successful can literally paralyze a person from doing anything.

What can procrastination do to you? Wreck your career, ruin
your family, destroy your chances for happiness or success, give
you bad health, and, yes, at its worst, kill you. In simple language,
procrastination can be downright expensive to you personally, to
your family, and to your friends. As one writer stated, "It can be a
vermin that will eat away at your professional effectiveness, steal your
valuable time, and keep you constantly disorganized and under great
emotional stress."

How can you conquer procrastination? First, tell yourself often
that you have a bad habit. Second, acknowledge that to overcome the
habit you must change the behavior that causes you to put things off.
Third, commit yourself to replacing the I'll-do-it-later attitude with an
I'll-do-it-now urge. Fourth, take positive steps on a continual basis to
make your commitment a reality.

Sir Isaac Newton's law of inertia tells us that a body at rest
tends to remain that way. As a result, it takes greater force to start
motion than to sustain it. When you procrastinate, you're at rest.
The only way to overcome that state is to get started. Once you
start moving, progress is more likely to continue as the momentum
builds up.

Here are some tips that will help you to get started. They'll also,
if practiced as a matter of routine, keep you moving in your battle
against procrastination. These hints will, in other words, help you fight
procrastination and win.

- Identify your important, high-value tasks, then put them in
  priority order. Focus your efforts on doing one job at a time
  in order of priority. Proceed from the most important to the
  least important.

- Set deadlines for everything you do. Plan what you want to
  do in advance and decide when you're going to do a task by
  hour and day, to the maximum extent that you can. Put your
  plan, schedule, and deadlines in writing.

- Do unpleasant things first, if at all possible. The sooner you
  get them out of the way, the better.

- Break a large or difficult task down into smaller parts. Take
  one part, finish it as fast as you can, and then move on to the
  next part.

- Give yourself a reward for completing a task by the deadline,
  which was imposed by someone else or set by yourself.

- Do a start-up task, such as buying a paint brush and the paint
  to get you started on painting the house that you've been

putting off doing, or purchasing the thread that you'll need to repair the dress you've been delaying fixing.

- Don't wait for inspiration; it may never come.
- Build yourself up. It's almost a certainty that you'll never do something if you think you can't do it.
- Avoid the perfection syndrome. Set a time limit to get something done, do your best the first time around, within the limit you've set, then go on to the next thing in accord with your priorities.
- Make every day count. Life is too short to waste time procrastinating. Develop the determination and willpower to do important things first and when they come up. Frequently, throughout every day, ask yourself, "Is this the best use of my time right now?" If the answer is "no" to what you're doing at the time, stop, and then start spending your time on a more important task.

In a nutshell, the best way to fight procrastination and win is never to have to battle with the behavior. Deter the behavior through strong preventative measures. Specifically:

- Make sure you know what you're trying to accomplish at all times. Have a purpose for everything that you do.
- Define your goals clearly and write them down.
- Set priorities and do things in the order of your priorities.
- Make doing things "now" a way of life; stop putting things off.

If you have a procrastination problem, admit it. Declare war on it. Attack the habit and defeat the enemy. Procrastination can be conquered, but like any other dangerous foe out to destroy your dreams, hopes, and chances for success in life, you must take positive action to overcome it. It's strictly up to you.

50

Time Management

Time is a man's most precious asset. All men neglect it; all regret the
loss of it; nothing can be done without it.
—Voltaire

Aside from a passion to write, which I've had for over fifty years,
I've also been devoted to using my time effectively in whatever I do. As
a matter of fact, from 1978 through 2000, I published a monthly time
management newsletter. The publication was distributed nationwide.
Why such a deep-seated interest in using my time wisely? Mostly, for
these reasons:

1. Because time is an extremely valuable but different kind of
   a resource.

2. Time is free. It's neither inflates or deflates. Furthermore,
   it's not subject to depression or recession.

3. It's the only facet of life where everyone is truly equal.
   Specifically, receiving the exact same amount of time.

4. Time is life. With enough time, one can do almost
   anything.

5. Time is personal. It's yours. No one can spend your time.

6. To manage time really means to manage yourself in such
   a way that you're able to accomplish your goals within the
   time available.

7. You really don't have enough time to do everything that
   could be done. No matter how much you do, there's always
   more you could do.

8. To control your time, it's necessary to think about what is
   the best use of your time.

9. There's always enough time to do what's most important.
   The challenge is to know what's important.

Be an effective time manager by doing the following:

- Clarify objectives.
- Plan your time.
- Control time use.
- Eliminate timewasters.

51

Must-Read Books for Young Adults

During my eighty-six years of life, I've read hundreds of books, most about leadership and management, motivated by my positions in the workplace. Consequently, at this point in my life, checking things off my short bucket list, I'm inspired to write this essay to share information that might be helpful to readers between ages eighteen and thirty-five. In addition, I felt the urge to pen this commentary from seeing the Foundation for a Better Life's television commercial "Pass It On." The three books highly recommended for young adults to read are: *Think and Grow Rich, How to Win Friends and Influence People,* and *The Seven Habits of Highly Effective People.*

Concerning *Think and Grow Rich,* it was first published in 1937 as a motivational, personal development, and self-help book by Napoleon Hill, as a suggestion from Scottish-American businessman Andrew Carnegie. While the title implies that the books deals with how to get rich, the author explains that the philosophy taught in the book can be used to help people succeed in all lines of work, and to do or be almost anything they want.

When Hill died in 1970, more than twenty million copies of the book had been sold. Furthermore, by 2011, over seventy million volumes had been purchased worldwide. *Businessweek* magazine's best-seller list ranked it the sixth best-selling paperback business book seventy years after it was published. Renowned business author John C. Maxwell has the publication on his "A Lifetime 'Must Read' Books List."

How to Win Friends and Influence People was released in 1936. Subsequently, it has been one of the best-selling self-help books ever printed. To date, over twenty-five million copies have been sold around the world. I first read the tome in my early twenties. Since then, I've perused it continually as a reminder to always try to do the right thing at the right time and for the right reason as I interacted with other people. Unequivocally, applying the principles and techniques set forth in the book aided me immensely throughout my life to the present day.

The Seven Habits of Highly Effective People, a business and self-help tome, was written by Stephen R. Covey and first published in 1989. As of this writing, more than thirty million copies in thirty-eight languages have been sold worldwide. The audio version of the publication has sold another 1.5 million copies. In *Seven Habits,* Covey presents an approach to being effective in attaining goals by aligning oneself to what he calls "true north" principles of a character ethic that he presents as universal and timeless. In 2011, *Time Magazine* listed *Seven Habits* as one of "The 25 Most Influential Business Management Books." President Bill Clinton read the book and invited Covey to Camp David to counsel him on how to integrate the book into his presidency.

Concluding, there's an old saying that says, "wisdom comes with age." I hasten to add a footnote to the adage: Obtain wisdom progressively, as fast as you can, by reading captivating, poignant, and stimulating books throughout your life. If you haven't read the three described, do it soon.

52

Famous Lifelong Learners

As a freelance writer for almost three decades, I've written articles on a multitude of different subjects. With few exceptions, the compositions have been about topics aimed toward reaching the largest audiences possible of men and women aged fifty plus. Recently, the thought occurred to pen an essay on well-known Americans who have pursued continuous learning throughout their lives. My purpose being to inspire readers to pursue learning as a continuous undertaking. Albert Einstein, the physicist and Nobel Laureate, expressed it well when he said, "Learning is not a product of schooling but the lifelong attempt to acquire it."

Wikipedia, the free online encyclopedia, says: "Lifelong learning, a colloquialism, is the ongoing, voluntary, and self-motivated pursuit of knowledge for either personal or professional reasons. Therefore, it not only enhances social inclusion, active citizenship, and personal development, but also self-sustainability, rather than competitiveness and employability."

Online, I came upon a blog entitled *25 Famous Lifelong Learners Who Inspire Us All*. Of the total, I selected the following well-known Americans to describe for readers to provide encouragement and inspiration to be lifelong learners.

1. George Washington. Washington was the first president of the United States. In addition, he was a statesman and commander in chief of the Continental Army during the American Revolution. He had little formal education. Unequivocally, he was self-taught.

2. Martin Van Buren. Van Buren was the eighth president of the United States. Furthermore, he served in the US Senate. His formal schooling ended at age thirteen.

3. Benjamin Franklin. Franklin was a statesman, inventor, printer, and a scientist, with other job skills on his resume. For years, he published *Poor Richard's Almanac.* He took

to learning on his own, working with other people who had experience, knowledge, and training.

4. Abraham Lincoln. Before becoming the sixteenth president of the United States, Lincoln was a self-educated lawyer, even though he had less than a year of formal schooling. Moreover, he didn't read excessively, but carefully studied each book he did read to be sure he completely understood it.

5. Stanley Kubrick. A famous US film producer and director, Kubrick had an irregular education and disliked going to school. He pursued self-learning all his life.

6. Arthur Ernest Morgan. A pioneer for flood control and dam construction methods, Morgan was a self-taught engineer. His education did not come from formal schooling, but he still went on to become president of Antioch College.

7. Harland Sanders. Given the military title of colonel by some unknown source, Sanders quit school in the sixth grade. After working in assorted dead-end jobs for years, upon reaching retirement age with little money, Sanders decided to better himself with self-education and, in the process over many years, opened the first Kentucky Fried Chicken (KFC) restaurant.

8. Malcolm X (his assumed name). Malcolm was an advocate for the rights of African Americans. He dropped out of school after a few years and was converted to Islam while in prison. While serving time, he spent hours each day reading, which resulted in him becoming self-educated. After he was released, he became an intellectual public figure for civil rights.

9. Quentin Tarantino. Tarantino is a film director and producer—ever heard of the *Pulp Fiction* or *Kill Bill*? At any rate, Tarantino left high school after several grades, and while working in a video store, learned how to make films.

10. Walt Disney. Disney, as most people know, before his death, created the world's most famous cartoon characters. He also founded the Walt Disney Company with theme parks in California and Florida, followed by like venues in major cities in foreign countries. What's interesting is that Disney taught himself how to draw through correspondence courses. Moreover, he continued to learn throughout his life.

11.   Abigail Adams. Adams the First Lady to John Adams, the second president of the United States and mother of John Quincy Adams, the sixth president of the United States, was well educated without ever attending school. She was tutored and learned to read. Friends said she simply had a desire to bolster her generous intellect.

12.   Ray Bradbury. Bradbury, a prolific science fiction writer with thirty books to his credit and over five hundred other works bearing his name, graduated from high school, but his impressive education is largely a product of independent reading.

13.   Bill Gates. Historical records reveal that Gates never graduated from a school of higher learning. Also, news releases say he recognized that continuous learning and self-improvement was essential to his success. Further, it is reported that he often picks up a copy of *Time* to read cover to cover, not just browsing but soaking up everything to ensure that he learn something he didn't know before.

14.   Alexander Graham Bell. It is well known that Bell invented the telephone and telegraph machine. What is not known by many is that he was self-taught. He only attended a few lectures in college, but continued to learn and experiment throughout his life.

15.   Walt Whitman. Whitman is one of America's most important poets. He was a reading lover. Furthermore, he taught himself to write, and even self-published a book.

Scientists have documented, in many studies, that lifelong learning benefits body, mind, and career. Therefore, all readers should actively engage and participate in continuous education.

For more information about the subject, the following websites are highly recommended:

- http://www.onlinecollege.org/2011/06/25-famous-lifelong-learner-who-inspire-us-all
- http://en.wikipedia.org/wiki/lifelng_learning
- http://www.bellevue.edu/ce/lifelong-learning-benefits-body-mind-and-career

53

Reading

Reading will give you lasting pleasure.
—Former First Lady Laura Bush

I was motivated to write this essay because March is National Reading Month. Additionally, inspiration to undertake the task came from research that revealed that many Americans aren't aware of the benefits of reading. Consequently, they seldom read or don't do it at all. Therefore, this composition's goal is to fill the two knowledge voids.

Concerning National Reading Month, in October 2007, the Women's National Book Association (WNBA) launched the initiative by hosting special reading events in nine major cities in the United States and the District of Columbia. Activities at the gatherings were designed to welcome folks and tell them about the movement. Items were sold and proceeds were used for various purposes, with some being donated to the US fund for United Nations International Children's Emergency Fund (UNICEF).

The mission of the WNBA is to:

- Increase public awareness of the joy and value of shared reading.

- Provide a time for reading groups to celebrate their accomplishments and plan.

- Provide opportunities for individuals to join an existing reading group or start a new one.

- Encourage libraries, bookstores, and organizations to host special reading group events.

Below are some interesting statistics about reading (all from *Publishers Weekly* magazine, except one as indicated):

- 53% of readers read fiction.

- 43% of readers read nonfiction.

- The favorite fiction category is mystery and suspense, at 19%.

- 55% of fiction is bought by women, 45% by men.

- 120,000 books are published each year in the United State (bookwire.com).

Regarding benefits of reading, researchers identified the following nine advantages (Source: http://www.rd.cin/health/benefits-of-reading/):

1. Gives muscle to your memory.

2. Bestows more staying power on your physical workouts.

3. Keeps your brain young.

4. Can melt away stress.

5. Enhances your vocabulary.

6. Improves empathy.

7. Encourages life goals.

8. Helps you feel more connected.

9. Can brighten your day.

While drafting this article, I was reminded of a blog I had read years before written by Leonard Kniffel, dated May 25, 2011, entitled *Reading for Life: Oprah Winfrey*. In the narrative, Winfrey is quoted as saying: "I don't believe in failure. Books were my path to personal freedom. I learned to read at age three, and soon discovered there was a whole world to conquer that went beyond our farm in Mississippi."

Also in the discourse, Kniffel adds this quote from Winfrey: "Because of his respect (speaking about her father) for education, every single week of my life that I lived with them I had to read library books and that was the beginning of the book club. Who knew? But I was reading books and had to do book reports in my own house. Now at nine years old, nobody wants to have to do book reports in addition to what the school is asking you to do, but my father's insistence that education was the open door to freedom is what allows me to stand today a free woman. When I was a kid and the other kids were home watching *Leave It to Beaver*, my father and stepmother were marching me off to the library. Getting my library card was like citizenship; it was like American citizenship."

Recently, I picked up a copy of *Time* magazine (November 7, 2016 edition). Much to my surprise, there was an article entitled "Read a Novel: It's Just What the Doctor Ordered," written by Sarah Begley. At the beginning, she wrote: "It's a well-established science that reading boosts vocabulary, sharpens reason and expands intellectual horizon." In the last paragraph of Begley's poignant composition, she wrote: "Even the greatest novel cannot, by itself, cure clinical depression, erase posttraumatic stress or turn an egomaniac into a self-denying saint. But it might ease a midlife crisis or provide comfort in time of grief."

Question? Do you have a reading habit? If your answer is no, suggest giving some thought to the benefits of reading.

54

The Writing Calling!

Who wants to become a writer? And why? Because it's the answer to everything . . . It's the streaming reason for living. To note, to pin down, to build up, to create, to be astonished at nothing to cherish the oddities, to let nothing go down the drain, to make something, to make a great flower out of life, even if it's a cactus.
—*Enid Bagnold*

Research reveals that many successful people are clandestine writers. Three in particular are Warren Buffet, Richard Branson, and Bill Gates. Buffet has described writing as a key way of refining his thoughts (and that is a man who reads and things a whole lot). Branson once said, "My most essential possession is a standard-sized notebook," which he uses for regular writing. Gates has described writing as a way to sit down and re-evaluate his thoughts during the day.

It's been documented in professional journals that "...getting significant ideas and thoughts down, using some media, alleviates the stress of losing something on your mind." One joke reportedly said by comedian, Mitch Hedberg: "I sit at my hotel, at night, I think of something that's funny, then I go get a pen and I write it down. Or if the pen's too far away, I have to convince myself that what I thought of ain't funny." Make no mistake, writing can be a most useful instrument to slow down the advent of dementia, as you grow older.

Investigations establish that writing regularly can produce many benefits. Among them are:

1. Makes you happier.

2. Leads to better thinking, coupled with more effective communicating with others.

3. Provides an outlet for coping with hard times and troubling situations.

4. Keeps your mind sharp.

5. Reduces mental distractions.

6. Enables mental distractions.

7. Facilitates the creation and maintenance of health moods, sense of well-being and greater thankfulness.

Remember these words of scriptures from the Bible:

"We write this to make our joy complete." (1 John 1:4)

"Now O king, issue the decree and put it in writing, so that it cannot be altered…so King Darius put the decree in writing." (Daniel 6: 8–9)

"Bind them on your fingers: write them on the tablet of your heart." (Proverbs 7:3)

Bottom line? Make writing a habit. It will be worth your effort and time.

55

Resiliency

Unequivocally, from Black Lives Matter to the election of a new president of the United States following eight years of the Obama administration, 2016 has been an electrifying year for all Americans. Nonetheless, based on historical records, not much has changed in terms of human experiences and the ways Americans cope with conditions and situations they encounter in their lives. Those facts form the basis for this essay, with the purpose of the composition being to discuss resiliency—an ability to recover from or adjust easily to change and misfortunes. Most folks will agree that it's tough to bounce back from setbacks. But as I write this commentary, I'm reminded of these quotes I've heard over the years:

"Tough times never last, but tough people do."

"Scars reminds us where we've been. They don't have to dictate where we're going."

"You never know how strong you are, until being strong is your only choice. It's hard to be a person who never gives up."

Then, coming from a Christian background, this verse of scripture from Ephesians 6:10-14:

> Finally, be strong in the Lord, relying on his mighty strength. Put on the whole armor of God so that you may be able to stand firm against the Devil's strategies. For our struggle is not against human opponents, but again rulers, authorities, cosmic powers in the darkness around us, and evil spiritual forces in the heavenly realm. For this reason, take up the whole armor of God so that you may be able to take a stand whenever evil comes. And when you have done everything you could, you will be able to stand firm. Stand firm, therefore, having fastened the belt of truth around your waist, and having put on the breastplate of righteousness.

With the foregoing background, the objective of this writing is to share important things I've learned about resiliency that might be beneficial to readers. Additionally, the catalyst for what's written comes from what Neil Rosenthal wrote in a column in the *Denver Post* dated January 21, 2016, entitled "Resilience Can Help You Redefine Yourself." Rosenthal, a licensed marriage and family therapist, and author of *Love, Sex and Staying Warm: Keeping the Flame Alive*, said many things in his extensive dissertation. The following are highlights of the contents of his work (all quotes):

- Be courageous and face your ordeals without losing your spirit. Resist the temptation to give up, and don't permit yourself to become embittered, jaded, angry, or hopeless.

- Create new, more-realistic goals. Disengage from goals that are no longer relevant, and instead set your sights on new visions for your future that are obtainable.

- View mistakes or setbacks as learning opportunities. Your mistakes are your teacher . . . Learn from your mistakes so you don't wind up repeating them.

- Keep your eye on the big picture. Look at things in perspective and develop a sense of proportion about what's truly important. In this regard, adversity can be a gift, keeping you focused on what on what you can do instead of what you can't control.

- Take good physical care of yourself. Eat healthy, exercise, go for therapy or medical checkups, get a massage, do yoga, and do other self-care activities.

- Be in control of your anguished emotions, so you don't alienate other people by taking out your hurt, anger, or unhappiness on them.

- Stay aware of the good things in your life. Having a sense of gratitude for what you have and what's right in your life will help you to stay hopeful and optimistic about your future.

In closing, certified personal and executive coach Valorie Burton expressed it well in her blog *After the Altar Call*. She quoted a verse from Psalm 30:5: "Weeping may endure for a night. But joy comes in the morning." Also, she added: "There is no doubt about it. No one is immune from tough times. But tough times don't last forever. Joy will come in the morning."

SOURCES:

http://www.biblereasons.com/resilence

http://www.afterthealtarcall.com/2011/10/seven-scriptures-to-inspire-resilience-during-t...1/21/2016
http://www.openbible.info/topics/resilience
http://www.beliefnet.com/Inspiration/Galleries/5-Things-Resilient-People-Do.aspx

56

Transcendental Meditation

My first experience with Transcendental Meditation (TM) occurred in the 1970s. Then, I was assigned to the Office of the Deputy Chief of Staff for Personnel, Headquarters Department of the Army in the Pentagon in Washington, DC. My job as a lieutenant colonel was as chief of the Alcohol Drug Abuse Prevention and Control Branch. The organization was a new Army entity created to develop and distribute plans and programs throughout the service for the care and treatment of soldiers who had become addicted to narcotics, mostly heroin, in Vietnam during the war. In addition to administrative personnel, my unit included a psychoanalyst, psychiatrist, and a social worker.

One day, my boss called me in to the office. He said, "Ben, I just read in a professional journal that a new technique called Transcendental Meditation can help people with drug problems." He added, "Stop what you're doing now and call to sign up for a class on TM." That's what I did and this summarizes the highlights of my experience.

After registering for the four days of training, I learned from research that TM was something anyone could do. The procedure was initially used in India in 1955 by Maharishi Mahesh Yogi, considered to be TM's founder and leader of the practice for over fifth years. The technique is practiced worldwide.

Regarding my TM learning, it was one-on-one with a certified teacher of the practice. He assigned me a mantra (a set of numbers, coupled with one or two words). Also, I was told not to reveal my mantra to anyone else. For twenty minutes, several times with the instructor, I went through the routine. That laid my TM foundation.

After completing the TM course, I returned to work and, with appropriate input from staff members, I edited the US Army's first comprehensive Alcohol and Drug Abuse Prevention and Control Program. Later, the document was published as a training manual and distributed worldwide for implementation.

Much research has been done that documents the range of personal benefits of TM—reduced anxiety and depression, improved memory and clearer thinking, reduced high blood pressure, less illness, a longer lifespan, and more harmonious relationships.

Make no mistake, TM works. Unequivocally, the practice is right for everyone, because it's effective. Try it! For more information about the technique, I highly recommend these two books, both written by Dr. Norman E. Rosenthal, MD: *Super Mind: How to Boost Performance and Live a Richer and Happier Life Through Transcendental Meditation* and *Transcendence: Healing and Transformation through Transcendental Meditation*.

Because I'm a Christian, every night while in bed, I read the Holy Bible. In addition, I meditate on his word. In addition, throughout each week I participate in Transcendental Meditation.

57

Addressing the Inevitable: Death

I've thought about writing an essay about death for years, but never did it for one reason or another. Nonetheless, recently I decided it was the time to touch the keyboard. The impetus to pen this article was a dream I had about "kicking the bucket." Foregoing notwithstanding, I believe that some readers might find the contents of this writing captivating and interesting, but most of all, useful in some way.

Beginning the task, my thoughts raced back to having read the need to plan for death. Consequently, I found several blogs on the subject that appealed to me. One was a May 25, 2011 weblog from *US News & World Report*, written by Philip Moeller, entitled "Living Well Should Include Planning for Death." In the work, Moeller reviews the book *You Only Die Once*, written by Margie Jenkins. Jenkins, he mentioned, also created a video called *Don't Slam the Door on Your Way Out*. Jenkins, about ninety years old, spent decades of her life counseling and conducting seminars and workshops around the country speaking about pre-death planning. Her objective, in Moeller's opinion, was: ". . . to bring dying and plans for dying into the conversations that people have with their spouses and family members."

Getting to another point, this quotation in Moeller's exposition about Jenkins fascinated me: "We plan for weddings, we plan for the birth of a baby, we plan for everything. We think you should plan for the end of life, too. There are just things that we think that you should think about doing, and many of them you can do now. We think people should put them into a file, give it a name, and tell their family what they're doing. Communication is so important. And you need to talk about this, and not whisper about it. It isn't going to go away, and we're all going to die someday."

Continuing to research, I came to a blog called "Planning for Death When You're Healthy." Written by Tara Parker-Pope, it appeared in the March 20, 2009 edition of *The New York Times*. The discourse was a review of Jane Brody's *Guide to the Great Beyond: A Practical*

Primer to Help You and Your Loved Ones Prepare Medically, Legally, and Emotionally for the End of Life. Reading, I was struck by this statement in the writing:

> *Everyone is willing to talk about nutrition and food and healthy Living. But people aren't so willing to talk about death. I really want to raise the public consciousness about the importance of having these kinds of discussions.*

Later, I was surprised to come upon a blog on the Internet from *The Guardian* entitled "Plan the death you want before it's too late." The article, written by Mayur Lakhani, chairman of the Dying Matters Coalition and the National Council for Palliative Care, had this moving introduction: "Talking about death is not easy. Most people avoid the topic. But ignoring the inevitable doesn't making it go away. All of us can benefit by talking openly about dying and discussing our wishes with those close to us . . . "

At the end of the discourse, Lakhani stated: "Dame Cicely Saunders, founder of the hospice movement, said: 'How people die remains in the memory of those whose live on. Preparing a good death is possible, but only if one's wishes are known. There is only one chance to get it right.'"

SOURCES:

http://www.money.usnews.com/money/blog/the-bestlife/2011/05/25/living-well-should-includ...

http://well.blogs.nytimes.com/2009/03/20/planning-for-death-when-youre-healthy/?php=true&t

http://www.theguardian.com/society/2012/may/15/plan-death-you-want-too-late

58

A Personal Note

The measure you give will be the measure you get, and still more be
given you.
—Mark 4:24

You've come to the end of *My Writings: Personal Essays*. Consequently, I thank you for taking the time to read or peruse what's set forth in this first volume of three. My hope is that something in this publication will be beneficial in some significant way in your life.

Unequivocally, I have been tremendously blessed by God to have so many experiences over six decades of life to create what's represented. Moreover, I was motivated to take on the task to give something back as part of my legacy.

As Denis Waitley wrote in a commentary in *The Answer: To Happiness, Health, and Fulfillment in Life: The Holy Bible*: "Even as we become self-reliant and take responsibility for planting the seed that will grow into the tree of our own success, we face an equal responsibility of planting a shade tree for the benefits of others. One of God's great rules for the harvest of success is that the crop we saw and reap must before the benefit of others, too . . ."

Lastly, please tell others about *My Writings: Personal Essays*. They too may become captivated, enlightened, and stimulated by its contents, while additionally receiving some worthwhile benefits.

Remember: "As each has received a gift, employ it for one another, as good stewards of God's varied grace; whoever speaks as one who utters oracles of God; whoever render it by the strength which God supplies; in order that in everything God may be glorified through Jesus Christ." (Peter 4:10-11)

About the Author

Hours after his birth, Ben Walton's biological mother dropped him off at an orphanage. It was nineteen years before she saw him again.

At the age of twelve, he ran away. He went to Florida to pick fruit as a migrant worker. For six months, he lived with illegal drugs, gambling, and prostitution. Then he returned home to the family who had taken him in after the orphanage went out of business.

Unable to adjust, he started playing hooky from school, became involved with boys who were stealing goods from stores, and was picked up by the police, but was not charged with a crime because of his age.

He took a test to enter the US Army at age fourteen, but failed. Afterward, he went to work full-time as a busboy and dishwasher at a hotel. Several years later, he retook the Army examination and passed it by two points. Thus, he entered the Army with an eighth-grade education.

Following basic training, he went to jump school to become a paratrooper, but flunked out. His next assignment was in Japan. There, in the army of occupation, he advanced through the ranks from private to sergeant.

When the Korean War broke out, he was among the first American troops sent into battle. Walton fought as an infantryman. He was a member of the combat unit that recaptured Yechon, the first South Korean city restored to friendly hands after the Korean War started in June 1950. While leading a platoon of thirty-six men, he was wounded. He received the Purple Heart for his injuries. Also, he was promoted to sergeant first class.

After the one-year tour in Korea, he returned to the United States, got married, and passed the high school general education development (GED) test, obtaining a high school diploma equivalent certificate. Then he went to the Field Artillery Officer Candidate School. Six months later, he graduated with distinction, number three in a class that started with eighty-six candidates; twenty-two finished the rigorous course.

As a commissioned Army officer, he had an illustrious military career. Highlights included: authoring the service's first comprehensive Alcohol and Drug Abuse Prevention and Control Program, while serving in the Pentagon as a staff officer; being nominated as a military aide to both the president of the United States and secretary of defense;

171

commanding an airborne field artillery battalion in Vietnam; completing the prestigious Naval Command and Staff Course at the Naval War College, graduating with distinction at that institution; completing the senior officers' course at the Industrial College of the Armed Forces; functioning as a military assistant to the deputy undersecretary of the Army for international affairs; serving as a Department of Defense advisor to the United States Panama Canal Treaty Negotiations Team, and being recognized by Ambassador Ellsworth Bunker, chief negotiator, for a stellar contribution to that group; directing a division artillery, and leading a team of American soldiers charged with coordinating combat support from United States forces to be provided to a South Korean field army in the event of a war with North Korea.

While on active duty, Walton was awarded the following military decorations: Purple Heart, Army Occupation Medal (Japan); Good Conduct Medal; Korean Service Medal; United Nations Service Medal; National Defense Service Medal with Oak Leaf Cluster; Expert Infantryman Badge; Combat Infantryman Badge; Army Commendation Medal with Third Oak Leaf Cluster; Bronze Star Medal with V Device and Second Oak Leaf Cluster; Legion of Merit with Fourth Oak Leaf Cluster; Meritorious Service Medal with Second Oak Leaf Cluster; Joint Services Commendation Medal; General Staff Identification Badge; Parachutist Badge; Aircraft Crewman Badge; Air Medal with Three Awards; Vietnam Campaign Medal with 60 Device; Vietnam Cross of Gallantry with Palm; and Vietnam Service Medal with Four Bronze Service Stars.

Walton retired from the US Army as a colonel. His second career began as administrative services director for a consortium of colleges and universities serving over 25,000 students in the Denver metropolitan area.

That was followed in order by these assignments: office services administrator for a major land development company; office services and facilities manager for a large law firm; assistant director of integrated technology services and office services manager at a private university; account manager for a Fortune 200 corporation; and distribution services manager for a no-load mutual funds company.

Walton was born in Highbank, Texas. He has a bachelor of general education degree from the University of Omaha, and a master of science degree from George Washington University. He is an accredited purchasing practitioner (APP), certified purchasing manager (CPM), certified administrative manager (CAM), certified manager (CM), and certified mail and distribution systems manager (CMDSM).

As a freelance writer, his articles on quality and participation subjects have appeared in many periodicals throughout the United States. He has served as president of the Colorado Front Range Chapter of the Association for Quality and Participation (CFRC-AQP).

Appendix A

Biography

US ARMY COLONEL BEN L. WALTON (RET.)

PERSONAL DATA:

Born: February 23, 1930, Highbank, Texas
Joined US Army February 4, 1948; Retired November 30, 1978

EDUCATION:

Bachelor of General Education, University of Omaha
Master of Science International Affairs, George Washington University
Military Service: 30 years

ENLISTED MAN:

Feb 48– May 48	PVT	Trainee	84th Tank Bn, Ft Knox, KY
Jun 48– Jan 49	PFC	Rifleman	25th Inf Regt, Ft Benning, GA
Feb 49– Jul 49	CPL	BAR Man	15th Inf Regt, Ft Benning, GA
Aug 49– Jun 50	CPL	Sqd Ldr	24th Inf Regt, Camp Gifu, Japan
Jul 50– Jul 51	SFC	Wpns Plat Ldr	24th Inf Regt, South Korea
Aug 51– Jun 53	SFC	Intel Sgt	25th Armor Inf Bn, Ft Hood, TX
Jul 53– Dec 53	SFC	Candidate	OCS, Ft Sill, OK (Distinguished Graduate)

COMMISSIONED OFFICER

| Jan 54–Jun 54 | 2LT | Instr | Ldrship Sch, Ft. Devens, MA |
| Jul 54–Feb 56 | 2LT/ | Asst XO | Btry B, 76th, FA, Ft Devens, MA |

FIRST LIEUTENANT

Mar 56–Sep 56	1LT	Btry XO	Btry B, 56th FA, Ft Carson, CO
Oct 56–Mar 57	1LT	Asst S3	HQ, 56th FA, Schwabach, Germany
Apr 57–Aug 57	1LT	LNO	HQ, 56th FA, Schwabach, Germany
Sep 57–Sep 58	1LT	Btry XO	Mort Btry, 8th Inf, Mainz, Germany
Oct 58–Jan 59	1LT	Btry FDO	Mort Btry, 8th Inf, Ft Riley, KS
Feb 59–Mar 60	1LT	Btry XO	Btry D, 7th FA, Ft Riley, KS
Apr 60–Feb 62	CPT	Btry CO	Btry B, 7th FA, Ft Riley, KS
Mar 62–Jul 62	CPT	S3	HQ, 7th FA, Ft Riley, KS
Aug 62–Jun 63	CPT	Student	IOCC, Ft. Benning, GA
Jul 63–Jul 64	CPT	Btry CO	HQ Btry, 3rd 80th Arty, Ft Sill, OK/Darmstadt, Germany
Aug 64–Mar 65	CPT/	S2	HQ, 36th FA Gp, Babenhausen, Germany

Major

Apr 65–Sep 65	MAJ	S4	HQ, 36 FA Gp, Babenhausen,
Oct 65–Jun 67	MAJ	MRO	HQ V Corps, Frankfort, Germany
Aug 67–Jun 68	MAJ/	Student	NWC, Newport, RI (Distinguished Graduate)

Lieutenant Colonel

Jul 68–Aug 68	LTC	Student	FAVOC, Fort Sill, OK
Sep 68–Feb 69	LTC	Bn CO	1st Bn/321st Arty, 101st ABN Div, RVN
Mar 69–Aug 69	LTC	Plans Off	J44, MACV, RVN
Oct 69–Jun 70	LTC	Chief,	C&SD/T/CAD, USAFAS, Ft Sill, OK

Elective Br

Jul 70–Jun 71	LTC	Student	ICAF, Washington, DC
Jul 71–Jun 72	LTC	Chief, PO Br.	ODCSPER, Washington, DC

DRUG ABUSE CONTROL DIV

Jul 72–May 73	LTC	Plans Off	ODCSLOG, Washington, DC
Jun 73–Mar 75	LTC/	Mil Asst to	ODUSA, Washington, DC

COL DUSA

Apr 75–Jun 75	COL Mil	Asst to	OASA (CW), Washington, DC

ASA (CW)

Aug 75–Jan 77	COL	CO	24th Inf DIVARTY, Hunter Army Airfield, GA
Feb 77–Mar 77	COL	Student	Defense Language Institute, Presidio of Monterey, CA
Apr 77–Apr 78	COL	CO	Combat Support Coordination Team #1, Wonju, South Korea
May 78–Nov 78	COL	Dep CO	USA Readiness Region, IX, Presidio of San Francisco, CA
Nov 78	COL	Retirement	

BADGES, DECORATIONS, AND MEDALS
Army Commendation Medal with 3 Oak Leaf Clusters
Bronze Star Medal with V Device and 2 Oak Leaf Clusters
Legion of Merit with 4 Oak Leaf Clusters
Meritorious Service Medal with 2 Oak Leaf Clusters
Joint Services Commendation Medal
Purple Heart
Army Occupation Medal (Japan) Good Conduct Medal
Korean Service Medal
United Nations Service Medal
National Defense Service Medal with Oak Leaf Cluster
Air Medal with 3 Oak Leaf Clusters

Vietnam Campaign Medal with 60 Device
Vietnam Cross of Gallantry with Palm
Vietnam Service Medal with 4 Bronze Service Stars
Expert Infantryman Badge Combat Infantryman Badge
Parachutist Badge
Aircraft Crewman Badge
General Staff Identification Badge

ADDITIONAL MILITARY HONORS:

Commendation for nomination as one of fourteen exceptional officers.

Recommended Army aide to President Richard M. Nixon by General Westmoreland, US Army chief of staff, 18 April 1972.

Commendation from Ambassador Ellsworth Bunker, chief US negotiator, US-Panama Canal Treaty Negotiations, Department of State, 2 September 1975.

Never criticize a man until you've walked a mile in his moccasins.
—American Indian proverb

Review Requested:

If you loved this book, would you please provide
a review at Amazon.com?

Lightning Source UK Ltd.
Milton Keynes UK
UKOW01n1504311017
311947UK00002B/31/P

9 781946 539854